# MEMORY

## A CONTRIBUTION TO EXPERIMENTAL PSYCHOLOGY

BY

## HERMANN EBBINGHAUS

PRIVAT DOCENT IN PHILOSOPHY AT THE UNIVERSITY OF BERLIN

(1885)

*'De subjecto vetustissimo
novissimam promovemus scientiam''*

TRANSLATED BY

## HENRY A. RUGER, Ph.D.

ASSISTANT PROFESSOR OF EDUCATIONAL PSYCHOLOGY, TEACHERS
COLLEGE, COLUMBIA UNIVERSITY

AND

## CLARA E. BUSSENIUS

PUBLISHED BY
Teachers College, Columbia University
NEW YORK CITY
1913

WINDHAM PRESS
CLASSIC REPRINTS

# TRANSLATORS' INTRODUCTION

The publication by Ebbinghaus of the results of his experimental investigation of memory (1885) marks the application of precise scientific method to the study of the "higher mental processes." By his invention of nonsense syllables as the material to be thus employed Ebbinghaus signalised the growing independence of experimental psychology from physics and physiology. For educational psychology his work is of especial importance because the field in which he worked was that of the ideational processes and because the problems which he attacked were functional and dynamic. The problem of the most efficient distribution of repetitions in committing material to memory may be taken to illustrate the identity in the nature of the questions investigated by him and those of especial interest to us to-day. Despite the fact that his experiments were performed only on himself and that the numerical results obtained are consequently limited in significance, his work stands as an embodiment of the essentials of scientific method. On account of its historical importance and also because of its intrinsic relation to present day problems and methods Ebbinghaus's investigation should be known as directly as possible by all serious students of psychology. To facilitate this acquaintance is the purpose of this translation.

The translators wish to acknowledge their indebtedness to Professors Edward L. Thorndike, Robert S. Woodworth, and E. W. Bagster-Collins of Columbia University, to Professor Walter Dill Scott of Northwestern University and to Mrs. H. A. Ruger for assistance in revising manuscript and proof.

## AUTHOR'S PREFACE

In the realm of mental phenomena, experiment and measurement have hitherto been chiefly limited in application to sense perception and to the time relations of mental processes. By means of the following investigations we have tried to go a step farther into the workings of the mind and to submit to an experimental and quantitative treatment the manifestations of memory. The term, memory, is to be taken here in its broadest sense, including Learning, Retention, Association and Reproduction.

The principal objections which, as a matter of course, rise against the possibility of such a treatment are discussed in detail in the text and in part have been made objects of investigation. I may therefore ask those who are not already convinced *a priori* of the impossibility of such an attempt to postpone their decision about its practicability.

The author will be pardoned the publication of preliminary results in view of the difficulty of the subject investigated and the time-consuming character of the tests. Justice demands that the many defects due to incompleteness shall not be raised as objections against such results. The tests were all made upon myself and have primarily only individual significance. Naturally they will not reflect exclusively mere idiosyncrasies of my mental organisation; if the absolute values found are throughout only individual, yet many a relation of general validity will be found in the relation of these numbers to each other or in the relations of the relations. But where this is the case and where it is not, I can hope to decide only after finishing the further and comparative experiments with which I am occupied.

# TABLE OF CONTENTS

# MEMORY

## CHAPTER I

## OUR KNOWLEDGE CONCERNING MEMORY

### Section 1. Memory in its Effects

The language of life as well as of science in attributing a memory to the mind attempts to point out the facts and their interpretation somewhat as follows:

Mental states of every kind,—sensations, feelings, ideas,— which were at one time present in consciousness and then have disappeared from it, have not with their disappearance absolutely ceased to exist. Although the inwardly-turned look may no longer be able to find them, nevertheless they have not been utterly destroyed and annulled, but in a certain manner they continue to exist, stored up, so to speak, in the memory. We cannot, of course, directly observe their present existence, but it is revealed by the effects which come to our knowledge with a certainty like that with which we infer the existence of the stars below the horizon. These effects are of different kinds.

In a first group of cases we can call back into consciousness by an exertion of the will directed to this purpose the seemingly lost states (or, indeed, in case these consisted in immediate sense-perceptions, we can recall their true memory images): that is, we can reproduce them *voluntarily*. During attempts of this sort,—that is, attempts to recollect—all sorts of images toward which our aim was not directed, accompany the desired images to the light of consciousness. Often, indeed, the latter entirely miss the goal, but as a general thing among the representations is found the one which we sought, and it is immediately recognised as something formerly experienced. It would be absurd to suppose that our will has created it anew and, as it were, out of nothing; it must have been present somehow

I

or somewhere. The will, so to speak, has only discovered
it and brought it to us again.

In a second group of cases this survival is even more striking.
Often, even after years, mental states once present in consciousness return to it with apparent spontaneity and without any act
of the will; that is, they are reproduced *involuntarily*. Here,
also, in the majority of cases we at once recognise the returned
mental state as one that has already been experienced; that is,
we remember it. Under certain conditions, however, this accompanying consciousness is lacking, and we know only indirectly that the " now " must be identical with the " then "; yet
we receive in this way a no less valid proof for its existence
during the intervening time. As more exact observation teaches
us, the occurrence of these involuntary reproductions is not an
entirely random and accidental one. On the contrary they are
brought about through the instrumentality of other, immediately
present mental images. Moreover they occur in certain regular
ways which in general terms are described under the so-called
laws of association.'

Finally there is a third and large group to be reckoned with
here. The vanished mental states give indubitable proof of their
continuing existence even if they themselves do not return to
consciousness at all, or at least not exactly at the given time.
Employment of a certain range of thought facilitates under certain conditions the employment of a similar range of thought,
even if the former does not come before the mind directly either
in its methods or in its results. The boundless domain of the
effect of accumulated experiences belongs here. This effect
results from the frequent conscious occurrence of any condition or process, and consists in facilitating the occurrence and
progress of similar processes. This effect is not fettered by
the condition that the factors constituting the experience shall
return *in toto* to consciousness. This may incidentally be the
case with a part of them; it must not happen to a too great
extent and with too great clearness, otherwise the course of the
present process will immediately be disturbed. Most of these
experiences remain concealed from consciousness and yet produce an effect which is significant and which authenticates their
previous existence.

## Section 2. Memory in its Dependence

Along with this bare knowledge of the existence of memory and its *effects,* there is abundant knowledge concerning the conditions upon which depend the vitality of that inner survival as well as the fidelity and promptness of the reproduction.

How differently do different *individuals* behave in this respect! One retains and reproduces well; another, poorly. And not only does this comparison hold good when different individuals are compared with each other, but also when different phases of the existence of the same individual are compared: morning and evening, youth and old age, find him different in this respect.

Differences in the *content* of the thing to be reproduced are of great influence. Melodies may become a source of torment by the undesired persistency of their return. Forms and colors are not so importunate; and if they do return, it is with noticeable loss of clearness and certainty. The musician writes for the orchestra what his inner voice sings to him; the painter rarely relies without disadvantage solely upon the images which his inner eye presents to him; nature gives him his forms, study governs his combinations of them. It is with something of a struggle that past states of feeling are realized; when realized, and this is often only through the instrumentality of the movements which accompanied them, they are but pale shadows of themselves. Emotionally true singing is rarer than technically correct singing.

If the two foregoing points of view are taken together— differences in individuals and differences in content—an endless number of differences come to light. One individual overflows with poetical reminiscences, another directs symphonies from memory, while numbers and formulae, which come to a third without effort, slip away from the other two as from a polished stone.

Very great is the dependence of retention and reproduction upon the intensity of the *attention* and *interest* which were attached to the mental states the first time they were present. The burnt child shuns the fire, and the dog which has been beaten runs from the whip, after a single vivid experience. People in whom we are interested we may see daily and yet not be able to recall the color of their hair or of their eyes.

Under ordinary circumstances, indeed, frequent repetitions are indispensable in order to make possible the reproduction of a given content. Vocabularies, discourses, and poems of any length cannot be learned by a single repetition even with the greatest concentration of attention on the part of an individual of very great ability. By a sufficient number of repetitions their final mastery is ensured, and by additional later reproductions gain in assurance and ease is secured.

Left to itself every mental content gradually loses its capacity for being revived, or at least suffers loss in this regard under the influence of time. Facts crammed at examination time soon vanish, if they were not sufficiently grounded by other study and later subjected to a sufficient review. But even a thing so early and deeply founded as one's mother tongue is noticeably impaired if not used for several years.

## Section 3. *Deficiencies in our Knowledge concerning Memory*

The foregoing sketch of our knowledge concerning memory makes no claim to completeness. To it might be added such a series of propositions known to psychology as the following: "He who learns quickly also forgets quickly," "Relatively long series of ideas are retained better than relatively short ones," "Old people forget most quickly the things they learned last," and the like. Psychology is wont to make the picture rich with anecdote and illustration. But—and this is the main point— even if we particularise our knowledge by a most extended use of illustrative material, everything that we can say retains the indefinite, general, and comparative character of the propositions quoted above. Our information comes almost exclusively from the observation of extreme and especially striking cases. We are able to describe these quite correctly in a general way and in vague expressions of more or less. We suppose, again quite correctly, that the same influences exert themselves, although in a less degree, in the case of the inconspicuous, but a thousand-fold more frequent, daily activities of memory. But if our curiosity carries us further and we crave more specific and detailed information concerning these dependencies and interdependencies, both those already mentioned and others,—if we put questions, so to speak, concerning their inner structure—our answer is silence. How does the disappearance of the ability to reproduce, forgetfulness, depend upon the length of time during which no repetitions have taken place? What proportion does the increase in the certainty of reproduction bear to the number of repetitions? How do these relations vary with the greater or less intensity of the interest in the thing to be reproduced? These and similar questions no one can answer.

This inability does not arise from a chance neglect of investigation of these relations. We cannot say that tomorrow, or whenever we wish to take time, we can investigate these problems. On the contrary this inability is inherent in the nature of the questions themselves. Although the conceptions in question—namely, degrees of forgetfulness, of certainty and interest —are quite correct, we have no means for establishing such degrees in our experience except at the extremes, and even then we cannot accurately limit those extremes. We feel therefore that we are not at all in a condition to undertake the investigation. We form certain conceptions during striking experiences, but we cannot find any realisation of them in the similar but less striking experiences of everyday life. *Vice versa* there are probably many conceptions which we have not as yet formed which would be serviceable and indispensable for a clear understanding of the facts, and their theoretical mastery.

The amount of detailed information which an individual has at his command and his theoretical elaborations of the same are mutually dependent; they grow in and through each other. It is because of the indefinite and little specialised character of our knowledge that the theories concerning the processes of memory, reproduction, and association have been up to the present time of so little value for a proper comprehension of those processes. For example, to express our ideas concerning their physical basis we use different metaphors—stored up ideas, engraved images, well-beaten paths. There is only one thing certain about these figures of speech and that is that they are not suitable.

Of course the existence of all these deficiencies has its perfectly sufficient basis in the extraordinary difficulty and complexity of the matter. It remains to be proved whether, in spite of the clearest insight into the inadequacy of our knowledge, we shall ever make any actual progress. Perhaps we shall always have to be resigned to this. But a somewhat greater accessibility than has so far been realised in this field cannot be denied to it, as I hope to prove presently. If by any chance a way to a deeper penetration into this matter should present itself, surely, considering the significance of memory for all mental phenomena, it should be our wish to enter that path at once. For at the very worst we should prefer to see resignation arise from the failure of earnest investigations rather than from persistent, helpless astonishment in the face of their difficulties.

## CHAPTER II

## THE POSSIBILITY OF ENLARGING OUR KNOWL-
## EDGE OF MEMORY

*Section 4. The Method of Natural Science*

The method of obtaining exact measurements—*i.e.*, numerically exact ones—of the inner structure of causal relations is,
by virtue of its nature, of general validity. This method, indeed,
has been so exclusively used and so fully worked out by
the natural sciences that, as a rule, it is defined as something
peculiar to them, as *the* method of natural science. To repeat,
however, its logical nature makes it generally applicable to all
spheres of existence and phenomena. Moreover, the possibility
of defining accurately and exactly the actual behavior of any
process whatever, and thereby of giving a reliable basis for the
direct comprehension of its connections depends above all upon
the possibility of applying this method.

We all know of what this method consists: an attempt is
made to keep constant the mass of conditions which have
proven themselves causally connected with a certain result; one
of these conditions is isolated from the rest and varied in a
way that can be numerically described; then the accompanying
change on the side of the effect is ascertained by measurement
or computation.

Two fundamental and insurmountable difficulties, seem, however, to oppose a transfer of this method to the investigation of
the causal relations of mental events in general and of those of
memory in particular. In the first place, how are we to keep
even approximately constant the bewildering mass of causal
conditions which, in so far as they are of mental nature, almost
completely elude our control, and which, moreover, are subject
to endless and incessant change? In the second place, by what
possible means are we to measure numerically the mental processes which flit by so quickly and which on introspection are so

7

hard to analyse? I shall first discuss the second difficulty in connection, of course, with memory, since that is our present concern.

## Section 5.  *Introduction of Numerical Measurements for Memory Contents*

If we consider once more the conditions of retention and reproduction mentioned above (§ 2), but now with regard to the possibility of computation, we shall see that with two of them, at least, a numerical determination and a numerical variation are possible.  The different times which elapse between the first production and the reproduction of a series of ideas can be measured and the repetitions necessary to make these series reproducible can be counted.  At first sight, however, there seems to be nothing similar to this on the side of the effects. Here there is only one alternative, a reproduction is either possible or it is not possible.  It takes place or it does not take place.  Of course we take for granted that it may approach, under different conditions, more or less near to actual occurrence so that in its subliminal existence the series possesses graded differences.  But as long as we limit our observations to that which, either by chance or at the call of our will, comes out from this inner realm, all these differences are for us equally non-existent.

By somewhat less dependence upon introspection we can, however, by indirect means force these differences into the open. A poem is learned by heart and then not again repeated.  We will suppose that after a half year it has been forgotten: no effort of recollection is able to call it back again into conscious· ness.  At best only isolated fragments return.  Suppose that the poem is again learned by heart.  It then becomes evident that, although to all appearances totally forgotten, it still in a certain sense exists and in a way to be effective.  The second learning requires noticeably less time or a noticeably smaller number of repetitions than the first.  It also requires less time or repetitions than would now be necessary to learn a similar poem of the same length.  In this difference in time and number of repetitions we have evidently obtained a certain measure for that inner energy which a half year after the first learning still dwells in that orderly complex of ideas which make up the poem. After a shorter time we should expect to find the difference greater; after a longer time we should expect to find it less. If the first committing to memory is a very careful and long continued one, the difference will be greater than if it is desultory and soon abandoned.

In short, we have without doubt in these differences numerical expressions for the difference between these subliminally persistent series of ideas, differences which otherwise we would have to take for granted and would not be able to demonstrate by direct observation. Therewith we have gained possession of something that is at least like that which we are seeking in our attempt to get a foothold for the application of the method of the natural sciences: namely, phenomena on the side of the effects which are clearly ascertainable, which vary in accordance with the variation of conditions, and which are capable of numerical determination. Whether we possess in them correct measures for these inner differences, and whether we can achieve through them correct conceptions as to the causal relations into which this hidden mental life enters—these questions cannot be answered *a priori*. Chemistry is just as little able to determine *a priori* whether it is the electrical phenomena, or the thermal, or some other accompaniment of the process of chemical union, which gives it its correct measure of the effective forces of chemical affinity. There is only one way to do this, and that is to see whether it is possible to obtain, on the presupposition of the correctness of such an hypothesis, well classified, uncontradictory results, and correct anticipations of the future.

Instead of the simple phenomenon—occurrence or non-occurrence of a reproduction—which admits of no numerical distinction, I intend therefore to consider from the experimental standpoint a more complicated process as the effect, and I shall observe and measure its changes as the conditions are varied. By this I mean the artificial bringing about by an appropriate number of repetitions of a reproduction which would not occur of its own accord.

But in order to realise this experimentally, two conditions at least must be fulfilled.

In the first place, it must be possible to define with some certainty the moment when the goal is reached—*i.e.*, when the process of learning by heart is completed. For if the process of learning by heart is sometimes carried past that moment and sometimes broken off before it, then part of the differences found under the varying circumstances would be due to this in-equality, and it would be incorrect to attribute it solely to inner differences in the series of ideas. Consequently among the different reproductions of, say, a poem, occurring during the process of its memorisation, the experimenter must single out one as especially characteristic, and be able to find it again with practical accuracy.

In the second place the presupposition must be allowed that the number of repetitions by means of which, the other condi-tions being unchanged, this characteristic reproduction is brought about would be every time the same. For if this number, under conditions otherwise equivalent, is now this and now that, the differences arising from varied conditions lose, of course, all significance for the critical evaluation of those varying conditions.

Now, as far as the first condition is concerned, it is easily fulfilled wherever you have what may properly be called learn-ing by heart, as in the case of poems, series of words, tone-sequences, and the like. Here, in general, as the number of repetitions increases, reproduction is at first fragmentary and halting; then it gains in certainty; and finally takes place smoothly and without error. The first reproduction in which this last result appears can not only be singled out as especially characteristic, but can also be practically recognised. For con-venience I will designate this briefly as the *first possible repro-duction.*

The question now is:—Does this fulfill the second condition mentioned above? Is the number of repetitions necessary to bring about this reproduction always the same, the other con-ditions being equivalent?

However, in this form, the question will be justly rejected because it forces upon us, as if it were an evident supposition, the real point in question, the very heart of the matter, and admits of none but a misleading answer. Anyone will be ready to admit without hesitation that this relation of dependence will be the same if perfect equality of experimental conditions is maintained. The much invoked freedom of the will, at least.

has hardly ever been misunderstood by anybody so far as to come in here. But this theoretical constancy is of little value: How shall I find it when the circumstances under which I am actually forced to make my observations are never the same? So I must rather ask:—Can I bring under my control the inevitably and ever fluctuating circumstances and equalise them to such an extent that the constancy presumably existent in the causal relations in question becomes visible and palpable to me?

Thus the discussion of the one difficulty which opposes an exact examination of the causal relations in the mental sphere has led us of itself to the other (§ 4). A numerical determination of the interdependent changes of cause and effect appears indeed possible if only we can realise the necessary uniformity of the significant conditions in the repetition of our experiments.

### Section 6.  *The Possibility of Maintaining the Constancy of Conditions Requisite for Research*

He who considers the complicated processes of the higher mental life or who is occupied with the still more complicated phenomena of the state and of society will in general be inclined to deny the possibility of keeping constant the conditions for psychological experimentation. Nothing is more familiar to us than the capriciousness of mental life which brings to nought all foresight and calculation. Factors which are to the highest degree determinative and to the same extent changeable, such as mental vigor, interest in the subject, concentration of attention, changes in the course of thought which have been brought about by sudden fancies and resolves—all these are either not at all under our control or are so only to an unsatisfactory extent.

However, care must be taken not to ascribe too much weight to these views, correct in themselves, when dealing with fields other than those of the processes by the observation of which these views were obtained. All such unruly factors are of the greatest importance for higher mental processes which occur only by an especially favorable concurrence of circumstances. The more lowly, commonplace, and constantly occurring processes are not in the least withdrawn from their influence, but we have it for the most part in our power, when it is a matter of consequence, to make this influence only slightly disturbing. Sensorial perception, for example, certainly occurs with greater or less accuracy according to the degree of interest; it is constantly given other directions by the change of external stimuli and by ideas. But, in spite of that, we are on the whole sufficiently able to see a house just when we want to see it and to receive practically the same picture of it ten times in succession in case no objective change has occurred.

There is nothing *a priori* absurd in the assumption that ordinary retention and reproduction, which, according to general agreement, is ranked next to sensorial perception, should also behave like it in this respect. Whether this is actually the case or not, however, I say now as I said before, cannot be decided in advance. Our present knowledge is much too fragmentary, too general, too largely obtained from the extraordinary to enable us to reach a decision on this point by its aid; that must be reserved for experiments especially adapted to that purpose. We must try in experimental fashion to keep as constant as possible those circumstances whose influence on retention and reproduction is known or suspected, and then ascertain whether that is sufficient. The material must be so chosen that decided differences of interest are, at least to all appearances, excluded; equality of attention may be promoted by preventing external disturbances; sudden fancies are not subject to control, but, on the whole, their disturbing effect is limited to the moment, and will be of comparatively little account if the time of the experiment is extended, etc.

When, however, we have actually obtained in such manner the greatest possible constancy of conditions attainable by us, how are we to know whether this is sufficient for our purpose? When are the circumstances, which will certainly offer differences enough to keen observation, sufficiently constant? The answer may be made:—When upon repetition of the experiment the results remain constant. The latter statement seems simple enough to be self-evident, but on closer approach to the matter still another difficulty is encountered.

## Section 7.  Constant Averages

When shall the results obtained from repeated experiments under circumstances as much alike as possible pass for constant or sufficiently constant? Is it when one result has the same value as the other or at least deviates so little from it that the difference in proportion to its own quantity and for our purposes is of no account?

Evidently not. That would be asking too much, and is not necessarily obtained even by the natural sciences. Then, perhaps it is when the averages from larger groups of experiments exhibit the characteristics mentioned above?

Again evidently not. That would be asking too little. For, if observation of processes that resemble each other from any point of view are thrown together in sufficiently large numbers, fairly constant mean values are almost everywhere obtained which, nevertheless, possess little or no importance for the purposes which we have here. The exact distance of two signal poles, the position of a star at a certain hour, the expansion of a metal for a certain increase of temperature, all the numerous coefficients and other constants of physics and chemistry are given us as average values which only approximate to a high degree of constancy. On the other hand the number of suicides in a certain month, the average length of life in a given place, the number of teams and pedestrians per day at a certain street corner, and the like, are also noticeably constant, each being an average from large groups of observations. But both kinds of numbers, which I shall temporarily denote as *constants of natural science* and *statistical constants*, are, as everybody knows, constant from different causes and with entirely different significance for the knowledge of causal relations.

These differences can be formulated as follows:—

In the case of the constants of the natural sciences each individual effect is produced by a combination of causes exactly alike. The individual values come out somewhat differently because a certain number of those causes do not always join the combination with exactly the same values (*e. g.*, there are little errors in the adjustment and reading of the instruments, irregularities in the texture or composition of the material examined or employed, etc.). However, experience teaches us that this fluctuation of separate causes does not occur absolutely irregularly but that as a rule it runs through or, rather, tries out limited and comparatively small circles of values symmetrically distributed around a central value. If several cases are brought together the effects of the separate deviations must more

and more compensate each other and thereby be swallowed up
in the central value around which they occur. And the final
result of combining the values will be approximately the same
as if the actually changeable causes had remained the same
not only conceptually but also numerically. Thus, the average
value is in these cases the adequate numerical representative of
a conceptually definite and well limited system of causal connections; if one part of the system is varied, the accompanying
changes of the average value again give the correct measure
for the effect of those deviations on the total complex.

On the other hand, no matter from what point of view statistical constants may be considered it cannot be said of them
that each separate value has resulted from the combination of
causes which by themselves had fluctuated within tolerably
narrow limits and in symmetrical fashion. The separate effects
arise, rather, from an oftimes inextricable multiplicity of causal
combinations of very different sorts, which, to be sure, may
share numerous factors with each other, but which, taken as a
whole, have no conceivable community and actually correspond
only in some one characteristic of the effects. That the value
of the separate factors must be very different is, so to say, self
evident. That, nevertheless, approximately constant values appear even here by the combining of large groups—this fact we
may make intelligible by saying that in equal and tolerably large
intervals of time or extents of space the separate causal combinations will be realised with approximately equal frequency;
we do this without doing more than to acknowledge as extant a
peculiar and marvellous arrangement of nature. Accordingly
these constant mean values represent no definite and separate
causal systems but combinations of such which are by no means
of themselves transparent. Therefore their changes upon variation of conditions afford no genuine measure of the effects of
these variations but only indications of them. They are of no
direct value for the setting up of numerically exact relations
of dependence but they are preparatory to this.

Let us now turn back to the question raised at the beginning
of this section. When may we consider that this equality of
conditions which we have striven to realise experimentally has
been attained? The answer runs as follows: When the average
values of several observations are approximately constant and

when at the same time we may assume that the separate cases
belong to the same causal system, whose elements, however, are
not limited to exclusively constant values, but may run through
small circles of numerical values symmetrical around a middle
value.

### Section 8.   The Law of Errors

Our question, however, is not answered conclusively by the
statement just made.  Suppose we had in some way found satisfactorily constant mean values for some psychical process, how
would we go about it to learn whether we might or might not
assume a homogeneous causal condition, necessary for their
further utilisation?  The physical scientist generally knows
beforehand that he will have to deal with a single causal combination, the statistician knows that he has to deal with a mass
of them, ever inextricable despite all analysis.  Both know this
from the elementary knowledge they already possess of the
nature of the processes before they proceed with the more
detailed investigations.  Just as, a moment ago, the present
knowledge of psychology appeared to us too vague and unreliable to be depended upon for decision about the possibility of
constant experimental conditions; so now it may prove insufficient
to determine satisfactorily whether in a given case we have to
deal with a homogeneous causal combination or a manifold of
them which chance to operate together.  The question is, therefore, whether we may throw light on the nature of the causation
of the results we obtain under conditions as uniform as possible
by the help of some other criterion.

The answer must be: This cannot be done with absolute certainty, but can, nevertheless, be done with great probability.
Thus, a start has been made from presuppositions as similar as
possible to those by which physical constants have been obtained
and the consequences which flow from them have been investigated. This has been done for the distribution of the single
values about the resulting central value and quite independently
of the actual concrete characteristics of the causes. Repeated
comparisons of these calculated values with actual observations
have shown that the similarity of the suppositions is indeed great
enough to lead to an agreement of the results. The outcome
of these speculations closely approximates to reality. It consists

in this,—that the grouping of a large number of separate values
that have arisen from causes of the same kind and with the
modifications repeatedly mentioned, may be correctly represented
by a mathematical formula, the so-called Law of Errors. This
is especially characterised by the fact that it contains but one
unknown quantity. This unknown quantity measures the relative
compactness of the distribution of the separate values around
their central tendency. It therefore changes according to the
kind of observation and is determined by calculation from the
separate values.

NOTE. For further information concerning this formula, which
is not here our concern, I must refer to the text-books on the
calculation of probabilities and on the theory of errors. For
readers unfamiliar with the latter a graphic explanation will
be more comprehensible than a statement and discussion of the
formula. Imagine a certain observation to be repeated 1,000
times. Each observation as such is represented by a space of
one square millimeter, and its numerical value, or rather its
deviation from the central value of the whole 1,000 observations,
by its position on the horizontal line $p$ $q$ of the adjoining
Figure I.
For every observation which exactly corresponds with the
central value one square millimeter is laid off on the vertical
line $m$ $n$. For each observed value which deviates by one
unit from the central value upward one square millimeter is
laid off on a vertical line to right of $m$ $n$ and distant one
millimeter from it, etc. For every observed value which deviates by $x$ units above (or below) the central value, one sq.
mm. is placed on a vertical line distant from $m$ $n$ by $x$
mms., to the right (or left, for values below the central value).
When all the observations are arranged in this way the outer
contour of the figure may be so compacted that the projecting
corners of the separate squares are transformed into a symmetrical curve. If now the separate measures are of such a
sort that their central value may be considered as a constant as
conceived by physical science, the form of the resulting curve is
of the kind marked $a$ and $b$ in Fig. I. If the middle
value is a statistical constant, the curve may have any sort of
a form. (The curves $a$ and $b$ with the lines $p$ $q$ include in each case an area of 1,000 sq. mms. This is strictly the
case only with indefinite prolongation of the curves and the lines
$p$ $q$, but these lines and curves finally approach each other so
closely that where the drawing breaks off only two or three sq.
mms. at each end of the curve are missing from the full number.)
Whether, for a certain group of observations, the curve has a

more steep or more flat form depends on the nature of those observations. The more exact they are, the more will they pile up around the central value; and the more infrequent the large deviations, the steeper will the curve be and *vice versa*. For the rest the law of formation of the curve is always the same. Therefore, if a person, in the case of any specific combination of observations, obtains any measure of the compactness of distribution of the observations, he can survey the grouping of the whole mass. He could state, for instance, how often a

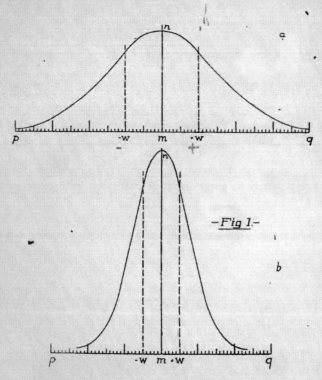

−Fig 1.−

deviation of a certain value occurs and how many deviations fall between certain limits. Or—as I shall show in what follows —he may state what amount of variation includes between itself and the central value a certain per cent of all the observed values. The lines $+w$ and $-w$ of our figure, for instance, cut out exactly the central half of the total space representing the observations. But in the case of the more exact observations of 1 *b* they are only one half as far from *m n* as in 1 *a*. So the statement of their relative distances gives also a measure of the accuracy of the observations.

Therefore, it may be said: wherever a group of effects may
be considered as having originated each time from the same
causal combination, which was subject each time only to so-
called accidental disturbances, then these values arrange themselves in accordance with the "law of errors."

However, the reverse of this proposition is not necessarily
true, namely, that wherever a distribution of values occurs
according to the law of errors the inference may be drawn
that this kind of causation has been at work. Why should
nature not occasionally be able to produce an analogous grouping in a more complicated way? In reality this seems only an
extremely rare occurrence. For among all the groups of numbers which in statistics are usually condensed into mean values
not one has as yet been found which originated without question
from a number of causal systems and also exhibited the arrangement summarised by the "law of errors."[1]

Accordingly, this law may be used as a criterion, not an absolutely safe one to be sure, but still a highly probable one, by
means of which to judge whether the approximately constant
mean values that may be obtained by any proceeding may be
employed experimentally as genuine constants of science. The
Law of Errors does not furnish sufficient conditions for such
a use but it does furnish one of the necessary ones. The final
explanation must depend upon the outcome of investigations to
the very foundations of which it furnishes a certain security.
That is why I applied the measure offered by it to answer our
still unanswered question: If the conditions are kept as much
alike as is possible, is the average number of repetitions, which
is necessary for learning similar series to the point of first
possible reproduction, a constant mean value in the natural
science sense? And I may anticipate by saying that in the case
investigated the answer has come out in the affirmative.

---

[1] The numbers representing the births of boys and girls respectively, as
derived from the total number of births, are said to group themselves in
very close correspondence with the law of errors. But in this case it is
for this very reason probable that they arise from a homogeneous combination of physiological causes aiming so to speak at the creation of a well
determined relation. (See Lexis, Zur Theorie der Massenerscheinungen
in der menschlichen Gesellschaft, p. 64 and elsewhere.)

## Section 9. Resumé

Two fundamental difficulties arise in the way of the application of the so-called Natural Science Method to the examination of psychical processes:

(1) The constant flux and caprice of mental events do not admit of the establishment of stable experimental conditions.

(2) Psychical processes offer no means for measurement or enumeration.

In the case of the special field of memory (learning, retention, reproduction) the second difficulty may be overcome to a certain extent. Among the external conditions of these processes some are directly accessible to measurement (the time, the number of repetitions). They may be employed in getting numerical values indirectly where that would not have been possible directly. We must not wait until the series of ideas committed to memory return to consciousness of themselves, but we must meet them halfway and renew them to such an extent that they may just be reproduced without error. The work requisite for this under certain conditions I take experimentally as a measure of the influence of these conditions; the differences in the work which appear with a change of conditions I interpret as a measure of the influence of that change.

Whether the first difficulty, the establishment of stable experimental conditions, may also be overcome satisfactorily cannot be decided *a priori*. Experiments must be made under conditions as far as possible the same, to see whether the results, which will probably deviate from one another when taken separately, will furnish constant mean values when collected to form larger groups. However, taken by itself, this is not sufficient to enable us to utilise such numerical results for the establishment of numerical relations of dependence in the natural science sense. Statistics is concerned with a great mass of constant mean values that do not at all arise from the frequent repetition of an ideally frequent occurrence and therefore cannot favor further insight into it. Such is the great complexity of our mental life that it is not possible to deny that constant mean values, when obtained, are of the nature of such statistical constants. To test that, I examine the distribution of the separate numbers represented in an average value. If it corresponds to the distribution found everywhere in natural science, where repeated observation of the same occurrence furnishes different separate values, I suppose—tentatively again—that the repeatedly examined psychical process in question occurred each time under conditions sufficiently similar for our purposes. This supposition is not compulsory, but is very probable. If it is wrong, the continuation of experimentation will presumably teach this by itself: the questions put from different points of view will lead to contradictory results.

## *Section 10. The Probable Error*

The quantity which measures the compactness of the observed values obtained in any given case and which makes the formula which represents their distribution a definite one may, as has already been stated, be chosen differently. I use the so-called "probable error" (P.E.)—*i.e.*, that deviation above and below the mean value which is just as often exceeded by the separate values as not reached by them, and which, therefore, between its positive and negative limits, includes just half of all the observational results symmetrically arranged around the mean value. As is evident from the definition these values can be obtained from the results by simple enumeration; it is done more accurately by a theoretically based calculation.

If now this calculation is tried out tentatively for any group of observations, a grouping of these values according to the "law of errors" is recognised by the fact that between the sub-multiples and the multiples of the empirically calculated probable error there are obtained as many separate measures symmetrically arranged about a central value as the theory requires.

According to this out of 1,000 observations there should be:

| Within the limits | Number of separate measures |
|---|---|
| $\pm \frac{1}{10}$ P.E. | 54 |
| $\pm \frac{1}{6}$ P.E. | 89.5 |
| $\pm \frac{1}{4}$ P.E. | 134 |
| $\pm \frac{1}{2}$ P.E. | 264 |
| $\pm$ P.E. | 500 |
| $\pm 1\frac{1}{2}$ P.E. | 688 |
| $\pm 2$ P.E. | 823 |
| $\pm 2\frac{1}{2}$ P.E. | 908 |
| $\pm 3$ P.E. | 957 |
| $\pm 4$ P.E. | 993 |

If this conformity exists in a sufficient degree, then the mere statement of the probable error suffices to characterise the arrangement of all the observed values, and at the same time its quantity gives a serviceable measure for the compactness of the distribution around the central value—*i.e.*, for its exactness and trustworthiness.

As we have spoken of the probable error of the separate observations, ($P.E._o$), so can we also speak of the probable error of the measures of the central tendency, or mean values, ($P.E._m$). This describes in similar fashion the grouping which would arise for the separate mean values ·if the observation of the same phenomenon were repeated very many times and each time an equally great number of observations were combined into a central value. It furnishes a brief but sufficient characterisation of the fluctuations of the mean values resulting from repeated observations, and along with it a measure of the security and the trustworthiness of the results already found.

The $P.E._m$ is accordingly in general included in what follows. How it is found by calculation, again, cannot be explained here; suffice it that what it means be clear. It tells us, then, that, on the basis of the character of the total observations from which a mean value has just been obtained, it may be expected with a probability of 1 to 1 that the latter value departs from the presumably correct average by not more at the most than the amount of its probable error. By the presumably correct average we mean that one which would have been obtained if the observations had been indefinitely repeated. A larger deviation than this becomes improbable in the mathematical sense—*i.e.*, there is a greater probability against it than for it. And, as a glance at the accompanying table shows us, the improbability of larger deviations increases with extreme rapidity as their size increases. The probability that the obtained average should deviate from the true one by more than 2½ times the probable error is only 92 to 908, therefore about 1/10; the probability for its exceeding four times the probable error is very slight, 7 to 993 (1 to 142).

# CHAPTER III

## THE METHOD OF INVESTIGATION

### *Section 11. Series of Nonsense Syllables*

In order to test practically, although only for a limited field, a way of penetrating more deeply into memory processes—and it is to these that the preceding considerations have been directed —I have hit upon the following method.

Out of the simple consonants of the alphabet and our eleven vowels and diphthongs all possible syllables of a certain sort were constructed, a vowel sound being placed between two consonants.[1]

These syllables, about 2,300 in number, were mixed together and then drawn out by chance and used to construct series of different lengths, several of which each time formed the material for a test.[2]

At the beginning a few rules were observed to prevent, in the construction of the syllables, too immediate repetition of similar sounds, but these were not strictly adhered to. Later they were abandoned and the matter left to chance. The syllables used each time were carefully laid aside till the whole number had been used, then they were mixed together and used again.

The aim of the tests carried on with these syllable series was, by means of repeated audible perusal of the separate series, to so impress them that immediately afterwards they could voluntarily just be reproduced. This aim was considered attained

---

[1] The vowel sounds employed were a, e, i, o, u, ä, ö, ü, au, ei, eu. For the beginning of the syllables the following consonants were employed: b, d, f, g, h, j, k, l, m, n, p, r, s, (= sz), t, w and in addition ch, sch, soft s, and the French j (19 altogether); for the end of the syllables f, k, l, m, n, p, r, s, (= sz) t, ch, sch (11 altogether). For the final sound fewer consonants were employed than for the initial sound, because a German tongue even after several years practise in foreign languages does not quite accustom itself to the correct pronunciation of the mediae at the end. For the same reason I refrained from the use of other foreign sounds although I tried at first to use them for the sake of enriching the material.

[2] I shall retain in what follows the designations employed above and call a group of several syllable series or a single series a "test." A number of "tests" I shall speak of as a "test series" or a "group of tests."

when, the initial syllable being given, a series could be recited at the first attempt, without hesitation, at a certain rate, and with the consciousness of being correct.

## Section 12. Advantages of the Material

The nonsense material, just described, offers many advantages, in part because of this very lack of meaning. First of all, it is relatively simple and relatively homogeneous. In the case of the material nearest at hand, namely poetry or prose, the content is now narrative in style, now descriptive, or now reflective; it contains now a phrase that is pathetic, now one that is humorous; its metaphors are sometimes beautiful, sometimes harsh; its rhythm is sometimes smooth and sometimes rough. There is thus brought into play a multiplicity of influences which change without regularity and are therefore disturbing. Such are associations which dart here and there, different degrees of interest, lines of verse recalled because of their striking quality or their beauty, and the like. All this is avoided with our syllables. Among many thousand combinations there occur scarcely a few dozen that have a meaning and among these there are again only a few whose meaning was realised while they were being memorised.

However, the simplicity and homogeneity of the material must not be overestimated. It is still far from ideal. The learning of the syllables calls into play the three sensory fields, sight, hearing and the muscle sense of the organs of speech. And although the part that each of these senses plays is well limited and always similar in kind, a certain complication of the results must still be anticipated because of their combined action. Again, to particularise, the homogeneity of the series of syllables falls considerably short of what might be expected of it. These series exhibit very important and almost incomprehensible variations as to the ease or difficulty with which they are learned. It even appears from this point of view as if the differences between sense and nonsense material were not nearly so great as one would be inclined *a priori* to imagine. At least I found in the case of learning by heart a few cantos from Byron's "Don Juan" no greater range of distribution of the separate numerical measures than in the case of a series of nonsense syllables in the learning of which an approximately equal time had been spent. In the former case the innumerable disturbing influences mentioned above seem to have compensated each other in producing a certain intermediate effect; whereas in the latter case the predisposition, due to the influence of the mother tongue, for certain combinations of letters and syllables must be a very heterogeneous one.

More indubitable are the advantages of our material in two other respects. In the first place it permits an inexhaustible amount of new combinations of quite homogeneous character, while different poems, different prose pieces always have something incomparable. It also makes possible a quantitative variation which is adequate and certain; whereas to break off before the end or to begin in the middle of the verse or the sentence leads to new complications because of various and unavoidable disturbances of the meaning.

Series of numbers, which I also tried, appeared impracticable for the more thorough tests. Their fundamental elements were too small in number and therefore too easily exhausted.

## Section 13. Establishment of the Most Constant Experimental Conditions Possible

The following rules were made for the process of memorising.

1. The separate series were always read through completely from beginning to end; they were not learned in separate parts which were then joined together; neither were especially difficult parts detached and repeated more frequently. There was a perfectly free interchange between the reading and the occasionally necessary tests of the capacity to reproduce by heart. For the latter there was an important rule to the effect that upon hesitation the rest of the series was to be read through to the end before beginning it again.

2. The reading and the recitation of the series took place at a constant rate, that of 150 strokes per minute. A clockwork metronome placed at some distance was at first used to regulate the rate; but very soon the ticking of a watch was substituted, that being much simpler and less disturbing to the attention. The mechanism of escapement of most watches swings 300 times per minute.

3. Since it is practically impossible to speak continuously without variation of accent, the following method was adopted to avoid irregular variations: either three or four syllables were united into a measure, and thus either the 1st, 4th, 7th, or the 1st, 5th, 9th . . . syllables were pronounced with a slight accent. Stressing of the voice was otherwise, as far as possible, avoided.

4. After the learning of each separate series a pause of 15 seconds was made, and used for the tabulation of results. Then the following series of the same test was immediately taken up.

5. During the process of learning, the purpose of reaching the desired goal as soon as possible was kept in mind as much as was feasible. Thus, to the limited degree to which conscious resolve is of influence here, the attempt was made to keep the attention concentrated on the tiresome task and its purpose. It goes without saying that care was taken to keep away all outer disturbances in order to make possible the attainment of this aim. The smaller distractions caused by carrying on the test in various surroundings were also avoided as far as that could be done.

6. There was no attempt to connect the nonsense syllables by the invention of special associations of the mnemotechnik type;  learning was carried on solely by the influence of the mere repetitions upon the natural memory. As I do not possess the least practical knowledge of the mnemotechnical devices, the fulfillment of this condition offered no difficulty to me.

7. Finally and chiefly, care was taken that the objective conditions of life during the period of the tests were so controlled as to eliminate too great changes or irregularities. Of course, since the tests extended over many months, this was possible only to a limited extent. But, even so, the attempt was made to conduct, under as similar conditions of life as possible, those tests the results of which were to be directly compared. In particular the activity immediately preceding the test was kept as constant in character as was possible. Since the mental as well as the physical condition of man is subject to an evident periodicity of 24 hours, it was taken for granted that like experimental conditions are obtainable only at like times of day.  However, in order to carry out more than one test in a given day, different experiments were occasionally carried on together

at different times of day. When too great changes in the outer
and inner life occurred, the tests were discontinued for a length
of time. Their resumption was preceded by some days of renewed training varying according to the length of the inter-
ruption.

## Section 14. Sources of Error

The guiding point of view in the selection of material and
in determining the rules for its employment was, as is evident,
the attempt to simplify as far as possible, and to keep as constant
as possible, the conditions under which the activity to be
observed, that of memory, came into play. Naturally the better
one succeeds in this attempt the more does he withdraw from
the complicated and changing conditions under which this activity
takes place in ordinary life and under which it is of importance
to us. But that is no objection to the method. The freely
falling body and the frictionless machine, etc., with which physics
deals, are also only abstractions when compared with the actual
happenings in nature which are of import to us. We can almost
nowhere get a direct knowledge of the complicated and the real,
but must get at them in roundabout ways by successive combinations of experiences, each of which is obtained in artificial,
experimental cases, rarely or never furnished in this form by
nature.

Meanwhile the fact that the connection with the activity of
memory in ordinary life is for the moment lost is of less importance than the reverse, namely, that this connection with the
complications and fluctuations of life is necessarily still a too
close one. The struggle to attain the most simple and uniform
conditions possible at numerous points naturally encounters
obstacles that are rooted in the nature of the case and which
thwart the attempt. The unavoidable dissimilarity of the
material and the equally unavoidable irregularity of the external
conditions have already been touched upon. I pass next to two
other unsurmountable sources of difficulty.

By means of the successive repetitions the series are, so to
speak, raised to ever higher levels. The natural assumption
would be that at the moment when they could for the first time
be reproduced by heart the level thus attained would always be
the same. If only this were the case, i.e., if this characteristic

first reproduction were everywhere an invariable objective sign of an equally invariable fixedness of the series, it would be of real value to us. This, however, is not actually the case. The inner conditions of the separate series at the moment of the first possible reproduction are not always the same, and the most that can be assumed is that in the case of these different series these conditions always oscillate about the same degree of inner surety. This is clearly seen if the learning and repeating of the series is continued after that first spontaneous reproduction of the series has been attained. As a general thing the capacity for voluntary reproduction persists after it has once been reached. In numerous cases, however, it disappears immediately after its first appearance, and is regained only after several further repetitions. This proves that the predisposition for memorising the series, irrespective of their differences of a larger sort according to the time of day, to the objective and subjective conditions, etc., is subject to small variations of short duration, whether they be called oscillations of attention or something else. If, at the very instant when the material to be memorised has almost reached the desired degree of surety, a chance moment of especial mental clearness occurs, then the series is caught on the wing as it were, often to the learner's surprise; but the series cannot long be retained. By the occurrence of a moment of special dullness, on the other hand, the first errorless reproduction is postponed for a while, although the learner feels that he really is master of the thing and wonders at the constantly recurring hesitations. In the former case, in spite of the homogeneity of the external conditions, the first errorless reproduction is reached at a point a little below the level of retention normally connected with it. In the latter case it is reached at a point a little above that level. As was said before, the most plausible conjecture to make in this connection is that these deviations will compensate each other in the case of large groups.

Of the other source of error, I can only say that it may occur and that, when it does, it is a source of great danger. I mean the secret influence of theories and opinions which are in the process of formation. An investigation usually starts out with definite presuppositions as to what the results will be. But if this is not the case at the start, such presuppositions form gradu-

ally in case the experimenter is obliged to work alone. For it
is impossible to carry on the investigations for any length of
time without taking notice of the results. The experimenter
must know whether the problem has been properly formulated
or whether it needs completion or correction. The fluctuations
of the results must be controlled in order that the separate
observations may be continued long enough to give to the mean
value the certainty necessary for the purpose in hand. Consequently it is unavoidable that, after the observation of the
numerical results, suppositions should arise as to general principles which are concealed in them and which occasionally give
hints as to their presence. As the investigations are carried
further, these suppositions, as well as those present at the beginning, constitute a complicating factor which probably has a
definite influence upon the subsequent results. It goes without
saying that what I have in mind is not any consciously recognised influence but something similar to that which takes place
when one tries to be very unprejudiced or to rid one's self of
a thought and by that very attempt fosters that thought or
prejudice. The results are met half way with an anticipatory
knowledge, with a kind of expectation. Simply for the experimenter to say to himself that such anticipations must not be
allowed to alter the impartial character of the investigation will
not by itself bring about that result. On the contrary, they do
remain and play a rôle in determining the whole inner attitude.
According as the subject notices that these anticipations are
confirmed or not confirmed (and in general he notices this during the learning), he will feel, if only in a slight degree, a sort
of pleasure or surprise. And would you not expect that, in
spite of the greatest conscientiousness, the surprise felt by the
subject over especially startling deviations, whether positive or
negative, would result, without any volition on his part, in a
slight change of attitude? Would he not be likely to exert
himself a little more here and to relax a little more there than
would have been the case had he had no knowledge or presupposition concerning the probable numerical value of the results?
I cannot assert that this is always or even frequently the case,
since we are not here concerned with things that can be directly
observed, and since numerous results in which such secret warping of the truth might be expected show evident independence

of it. All I can say is, we must expect something of the sort from our general knowledge of human nature, and in any investigations in which the inner attitude is of very great importance, as for example in experiments on sense perception, we must give special heed to its misleading influence.

It is evident how this influence in general makes itself felt. With average values it would tend to level the extremes; where especially large or small numbers are expected it would tend to further increase or decrease the values. This influence can only be avoided with certainty when the tests are made by two persons working together, one of whom acts as subject for a certain time without raising any questions concerning the purpose or the result of the investigations. Otherwise help can be obtained only by roundabout methods, and then, probably, only to a limited extent. The subject, as I myself always did, can conceal from himself as long as possible the exact results. The investigation can be extended in such a way that the upper limits of the variables in question are attained. In this way, whatever warping of the truth takes place becomes relatively more difficult and unimportant. Finally, the subject can propose many problems which will appear to be independent of each other in the hope that, as a result, the true relation of the interconnected mental processes will break its way through.

To what extent the sources of error mentioned have affected the results given below naturally cannot be exactly determined. The absolute value of the numbers will doubtless be frequently influenced by them, but as the purpose of the tests could never have been the precise determination of absolute values, but rather the attainment of comparative results (especially in the numerical sense) and relatively still more general results, there is no reason for too great anxiety. In one important case (§ 38) I could directly convince myself that the exclusion of all knowledge concerning the character of the results brought about no change; in another case where I myself could not eliminate a doubt I called especial attention to it. In any case he who is inclined *a priori* to estimate very highly the unconscious influence of secret wishes on the total mental attitude will also have to take into consideration that the secret wish to find objective truth and not with disproportionate toil to place the creation of his own fancy upon feet of clay—that this wish,

I say, may also claim a place in the complicated mechanism of
these possible influences.

## Section 15.  Measurement of Work Required

The number of repetitions which were necessary for memorising a series up to the first possible reproduction was not
originally determined by counting, but indirectly by measuring
in seconds the time that was required to memorise it.  My purpose was in this way to avoid the distraction necessarily connected
with counting; and I could assume that there was a proportional
relation existing between the times and the number of repetitions
occurring at any time in a definite rhythm.  We could scarcely
expect this proportionality to be perfect, since, when only the
time is measured, the moments of hesitation and reflection are
included, which is not true when the repetitions are counted.
Difficult series in which hesitation will occur relatively more
frequently, will, by the method of time measurement, get comparatively greater numbers, the easier series will get comparatively smaller numbers than when the repetitions are counted.
But with larger groups of series a tolerably equal distribution
of difficult and equal series may be taken for granted.  Consequently the deviations  from  proportionality will compensate
themselves in a similar manner in the case of each group.

When, for certain tests, the direct counting of the repetitions
became necessary, I proceeded in the following manner.  Little
wooden buttons measuring about 14 mms. in diameter and 4
mms. at their greatest thickness were strung on a cord which
would permit of easy displacement and yet heavy enough to
prevent accidental slipping.  Each tenth piece was black; the
others had their natural color.  During the memorisation the
cord was held in the hand and at each new repetition a piece
was displaced some centimeters from left to right.  When the
series could be recited, a glance at the cord, since it was divided
into tens, was enough to ascertain the number of repetitions that
had been necessary.  The manipulation required so little attention that in the mean values of the time used (which was always
tabulated at the same time) no lengthening could be noted as
compared with earlier tests.

By means of this simultaneous measurement of time and repe-

titions incidental opportunity was afforded for verifying and
more accurately defining that which had been foreseen and
which has just been explained with regard to their interrelation.
When the prescribed rhythm of 150 strokes per minute was precisely maintained, each syllable would take 0.4 second; and when
the simple reading of the series was interrupted by attempts
to recite it by heart, the unavoidable hesitations would lengthen
the time by small but fairly uniform amounts. This, however,
did not hold true with any exactness; on the contrary, the following modifications appeared.

When the direct reading of the series predominated, a certain
forcing, an acceleration of the rhythm, occurred which, without
coming to consciousness, on the whole lowered the time for each
syllable below the standard of 0.4 sec.

When there was interchange between reading and reciting,
however, the lengthening of the time was not in general constant,
but was greater with the longer series. In this case, since the
difficulty increases very rapidly with increasing length of the
series, there occurs a slowing of the tempo, again involuntary
and not directly noticeable. Both are illustrated by the following table.

| Series of 16 syllables, for the most part read | Each syllable required the average time of | Number of series | Number of syllables |
|---|---|---|---|
| 8 times | 0.398 sec. | 60 | 960 |
| 16 " | 0.399 " | 108 | 1728 |

| Series of X syllables | Were in part read, in part recited on an average Y times | Each syllable required an average time of Z secs. | Number of series | Number of syllables |
|---|---|---|---|---|
| X= | Y= | Z= | | |
| 12 | 18 | 0.416 | 63 | 756 |
| 16 | 31 | 0.427 | 252 | 4032 |
| 24 | 45 | 0.438 | 21 | 504 |
| 36 | 56 | 0.459 | 14 | 504 |

As soon as this direction of deviation from exact proportionality was noticed there appeared in the learning a certain
conscious reaction against it.

Finally, it appeared that the probable error of the time measurements was somewhat larger than that of the repetitions.
This relation is quite intelligible in the light of the explanations
given above.  In the case of the time measurements the larger
values, which naturally occurred with the more difficult series,
were relatively somewhat greater than in the case of the number
of repetitions, because relatively they were for the most part
lengthened by the hesitations; conversely, the smaller times were
necessarily somewhat smaller relatively than the number of
repetitions, because in general they corresponded to the easier
series.  The distribution of the values in the case of the times
is therefore greater than that of the values in the case of the
repetitions.

The differences between the two methods of reckoning are,
as is readily seen, sufficiently large to lead to different results
in the case of investigations seeking a high degree of exactness.
That is not the case with the results as yet obtained; it is therefore immaterial whether the number of seconds is used or that
of the repetitions.

Decision cannot be given *a priori* as to which method of
measurement is more correct—*i.e.,* is the more adequate measure
of the mental work expended.  It can be said that the impressions are due entirely to the repetitions, they are the thing
that counts; it can be said that a hesitating repetition is just as
good as a simple fluent reproduction of the line, and that both
are to be counted equally.  But on the other hand it may be
doubted that the moments of recollection are merely a loss.
In any case a certain display of energy takes place in them:
on the one hand, a very rapid additional recollection of the immediately preceding words occurs, a new start, so to speak, to get
over the period of hesitation; on the other hand, there is heightened attention to the passages following.  If with this, as is
probable, a firmer memorisation of the series takes place, then
these moments have a claim upon consideration which can only
be given to them through the measurement of the times.

Only when a considerable difference in the results of the two
kinds of tabulation appears will it be possible to give one the
preference over the other.  That one will then be chosen which
gives the simpler formulation of the results in question.

## Section 16.  Periods of the Tests

The tests were made in two periods, in the years 1879-80 and 1883-84, and extended each over more than a year.  During a long time preliminary experiments of a similar nature had preceded the definite tests of the first period, so that, for all results communicated, the time of increasing skill may be considered as past.  At the beginning of the second period I was careful to give myself renewed training.  This temporal distribution of the tests with a separating interval of more than three years gives the desired possibility of a certain mutual control of most of the results.  Frankly, the tests of the two periods are not strictly comparable.  In the case of the tests of the first period, in order to limit the significance of the first fleeting grasp[1] of the series in moments of special concentration, it was decided to study the series until two successive faultless reproductions  were possible.  Later I abandoned this method, which only incompletely accomplished its purpose, and kept to the first fluent reproduction.  The earlier method evidently in many cases resulted in a somewhat longer period of learning.  In addition there was a difference in the hours of the day appointed for the tests.  Those of the later period all occurred in the afternoon hours between one and three o'clock; those of the earlier period were unequally divided between the hours of 10-11 A. M., 11-12 A. M., and 6-8 P. M., which for the sake of brevity I shall designate A, B, and C.

---

[1] Described in § 14.

# CHAPTER IV

## THE UTILITY OF THE AVERAGES OBTAINED

### Section 17.  Grouping of the Results of the Tests

The first question which awaits an answer from the investigations carried out in the manner described is, as explained in sections 7 and 8, that of the nature of the averages obtained. Are the lengths of time required for memorising series of a certain length, under conditions as nearly identical as possible, grouped in such a way that we may be justified in considering their average values as measures in the sense of physical science, or are they not?

If the tests are made in the way described above, namely, so that several series are always memorised in immediate succession, such a type of grouping of the time records could scarcely be expected. For, as the time devoted to learning at a given sitting becomes extended, certain variable conditions in the separate series come into play, the fluctuations of which we could not very well expect, from what we know of their nature, to be distributed symmetrically around a mean value. Accordingly the grouping of the results must be an asymmetrical one and cannot correspond to the " law of error." Such conditions are the fluctuations of attention and the decreasing mental freshness, which, at first very quickly and then more and more slowly, gives way to a certain mental fatigue. There are no limits, so to speak, to the slowing down of the learning processes caused by unusual distractions; as a result of these the time for learning a series may occasionally be increased to double that of its average value or more. The opposite effect, that of an unusual exertion, cannot in the very nature of the case overstep a certain limit. It can never reduce the learning time to zero.

If, however, groups of series equal in number and learned in immediate succession are taken, these disturbing influences

34

may be considered to have disappeared or practically so. The decrease in mental vigour in one group will be practically the same as that in another. The positive and negative fluctuations of attention which under like conditions occur during a quarter or half hour are approximately the same from day to day. All that is necessary to ask, then, is: Do the times necessary for learning equal groups of series exhibit the desired distribution?

I can answer this question in the affirmative with sufficient certainty. The two longest series, obtained under conditions similar to each other, which I possess, are, to be sure, not large in the above-mentioned theoretical sense; they suffer, moreover, from the disadvantage that they originated at times separated by comparatively long intervals during which there were necessarily many changes in the conditions. In spite of this, their grouping comes as near as could be expected to the one demanded by the theory.

The first test series taken during the years 1879-80 comprises 92 tests. Each test consisted in memorising eight series of 13 syllables each, which process of learning was continued until two reproductions of each series were possible. The time required for all eight series taken together including the time for the two reproductions (but of course not for the pauses, see p. 25, 4) amounted to an average of 1,112 seconds with a probable error of observation of ± 76. The fluctuations of the results were, therefore, very significant: only half of the numbers obtained fell between the limits 1,036 and 1,188, the other half was distributed above and below these limits. In detail the grouping of the numbers is as follows:

| Within the limits | *i.e.* within the deviation | Number of deviations | |
|---|---|---|---|
| | | By actual count | Calculated from theory |
| 1/6 P.E. | ± 7 | 6 | 5 |
| 1/3 P.E. | ± 12 | 10 | 8.2 |
| 1/2 P.E. | ± 19 | 13 | 12.3 |
| 1/2 P.E. | ± 38 | 30 | 24.3 |
| P.E. | ± 76 | 45 | 46.0 |
| 1½ P.E. | ± 114 | 61 | 63.4 |
| 2 P.E. | ± 152 | 73 | 75.6 |
| 2½ P.E. | ± 190 | 84 | 83.6 |
| 3 P.E. | ± 228 | 88 | 88.0 |

In the interval, ¼ P.E. to ½ P.E., there occurs a slight piling up of values which is compensated for by a greater lack in the succeeding interval, ½ P.E. to P.E. Apart from this, the correspondence between the calculated and the actual results is satisfactory. The symmetry of the distribution leaves something to be desired. The values below the average preponderate a little in number, those above preponderate a little in amount of deviation: only two of the largest eight deviations are below the mean value. The influence of attention referred to above, the fluctuations of which in the separate series show greater deviations toward the upper limit than toward the lower, has not, therefore, been quite compensated by the combination of several series.

The correctness of the observations and the correspondence of their distributions with the one theoretically demanded are greatly improved in the second large series of tests. The latter comprises the results of 84 series of tests taken during the years 1883-84. Each test consisted in memorising six series of 16 syllables each, carried on in each case to the first errorless reproduction. The whole time necessary for this amounted to 1,261 seconds with the probable error of observation of ± 48.4— i.e., half of all the 84 numbers fell within the limits 1,213-1,309. The exactness of the observations thus had greatly increased as compared with the former series of tests :[1]

The interval included by the probable error amounts to only 7½ per cent of the mean value as against 14 per cent in the earlier tests. In detail the numbers are distributed as follows:

---

[1] Of course, the exactness obtained here cannot stand comparison with physical measurements, but it can very well be compared with physiological ones, which would naturally be the first to be thought of in this connection. To the most exact of physiological measurements belong the last determinations of the speed of nervous transmission made by Helmholtz and Baxt. One record of these researches published as an illustration of their accuracy (Mon. Ber. d. Berl. Akad. 1870, S. 191) after proper calculation gives a mean value of 4.268 with the probable error of observation, 0.101. The interval it includes amounts, therefore, to 5 per cent of the mean value. All former determinations are much more inaccurate. In the case of the most accurate test-series of the first measurements made by Helmholtz, that interval amounts to about 50 per cent of the mean value (*Arch. f. Anat. u.. Physiol.* 1850, S. 340). Even Physics, in the case of its pioneer investigations, has often been obliged to put up with a less degree of accuracy in its numerical results. In the case of his first determinations of the mechanical equivalent of heat Joule found the number 838, with a probable error of observation of 97. (*Phil. Mag.*, 1843, p. 435 ff.)

| Within the limits | *i.e.*, within the deviation | Number of deviations | |
|---|---|---|---|
| | | By actual count | Calculated from theory |
| $\frac{1}{10}$ P.E. | ± 4 | 4 | 4.5 |
| $\frac{1}{4}$ P.E. | ± 8 | 7 | 7.6 |
| $\frac{1}{4}$ P.E. | ± 12 | 12 | 11.3 |
| $\frac{1}{2}$ P.E. | ± 24 | 23 | 22.2 |
| P.E. | ± 48 | 44 | 42.0 |
| 1$\frac{1}{2}$ P.E. | ± 72 | 57 | 57.8 |
| 2 P.E. | ± 96 | 68 | 69.0 |
| 2$\frac{1}{2}$ P.E. | ± 121 | 75 | 76.0 |
| 3 P.E. | ± 145 | 81 | 80.0 |

The symmetry of distribution is here satisfactorily maintained apart from the numbers, which are unimportant on account of their smallness.

| Within the limits | Deviations | |
|---|---|---|
| | Above | Below |
| $\frac{1}{6}$ P.E. | 5 | 2 |
| $\frac{1}{4}$ P.E. | 7 | 5 |
| $\frac{1}{2}$ P.E. | 13 | 10 |
| P.E. | 20 | 24 |
| 1$\frac{1}{2}$ P.E. | 28 | 29 |
| 2 P.E. | 34 | 34 |
| 2$\frac{1}{2}$ P.E. | 37 | 38 |
| 3 P.E. | 40 | 41 |

The deviation which is greatest absolutely is toward the lower limit.

If several of our series of syllables were combined into groups and then memorised separately, the length of time necessary to memorise a whole group varied greatly, to be sure, when repeated tests were taken; but, in spite of this, when taken as a whole they varied in a manner similar to that of the measures of the ideally homogeneous processes of natural science, which also vary from each other. So, at least in experimental fashion, it is allowable to use the mean values obtained from the numerical results for the various tests in order to establish the existence of causal relations just as natural science does that by means of its constants.

The number of series of syllables which is to be combined into a single group, or test, is naturally indeterminate. It must be expected, however, that as the number increases, the correspondence between the distribution of the times actually found and those calculated in accordance with the law of errors will be greater. In practice the attempt will be made to increase the number to such a point that further increase and the closer correspondence resulting will no longer compensate for the time required. If the number of the series in a given test is lessened, the desired correspondence will also presumably decrease. However, it is desirable that even then the approximation to the theoretically demanded distribution remain perceptible.

Even this requirement is fulfilled by the numerical values obtained. In the two largest series of tests just described, I have examined the varying length of time necessary for the memorisation of the first half of each test. In the older series, these are the periods required by each 4 series of syllables, in the more recent series the periods required by each 3 of them taken together. The results are as follows:

1. In the former series: mean value $(m) = 533$ $(P.E._o) = \pm 51$.

DISTRIBUTION OF THE SEPARATE VALUES

| Within the limits | *i.e.,* within the deviation | Number of deviations | | Of these deviations there occur | |
|---|---|---|---|---|---|
| | | By actual count | Calculated from theory | Below | Above |
| $\frac{1}{10}$ P.E. | $\pm$ 5 | 2 | 5.0 | 2 | 0 |
| $\frac{1}{6}$ P.E. | $\pm$ 8 | 4 | 8.2 | 3 | 1 |
| $\frac{1}{4}$ P.E. | $\pm$ 12 | 6 | 12.3 | 4 | 2 |
| $\frac{1}{2}$ P.E. | $\pm$ 25 | 21 | 24.3 | 9 | 12 |
| P.E. | $\pm$ 51 | 48 | 46.0 | 24 | 24 |
| $1\frac{1}{2}$ P.E. | $\pm$ 76 | 61 | 63.4 | 30 | 31 |
| 2 P.E. | $\pm$ 102 | 76 | 75.6 | 37 | 39 |
| $2\frac{1}{2}$ P.E. | $\pm$ 127 | 85 | 83.6 | 42 | 43 |
| 3 P.E. | $\pm$ 153 | 89 | 88.0 | 45 | 44 |

2. In the later series: $m = 620$, P.E.$_o = \pm 44$.

DISTRIBUTION OF THE SEPARATE VALUES

| Within the limits | *i.e.*, within the deviation | Number of deviations | | Of these deviations there occur | |
|---|---|---|---|---|---|
| | | By actual count | Calculated from theory | Below | Above |
| $\frac{1}{10}$ P.E. | ± 4 | 3 | 4.5 | 1 | 2 |
| $\frac{1}{6}$ P.E. | ± 7 | 5 | 7.6 | 3 | 2 |
| $\frac{1}{4}$ P.E. | ± 11 | 11 | 11.3 | 6 | 5 |
| $\frac{1}{2}$ P.E. | ± 22 | 25 | 22.2 | 13 | 12 |
| 1 P.E. | ± 44 | 44 | 42.0 | 21 | 23 |
| $1\frac{1}{2}$ P.E. | ± 66 | 56 | 57.8 | 29 | 27 |
| 2 P.E. | ± 88 | 71 | 69.0 | 38 | 33 |
| $2\frac{1}{2}$ P.E. | ± 110 | 76 | 76.0 | 41 | 35 |
| 3 P.E. | ± 132 | 79 | 80.0 | 42 | 37 |

By both tables the supposition mentioned above of the existence of a less perfect but still perceptible correspondence between the observed and calculated distribution of the numbers is well confirmed.

Exactly the same approximate correspondence must be presupposed if, instead of decreasing the number of series combined into a test, the total number of tests is made smaller. In this case also I will add some confirmatory summaries.

I possess two long test series, made at the time of the earlier tests, which were obtained under the same conditions as the above mentioned series but at the later times of the day, B. and C.

One of these, B, comprised 39 tests of 6 series each, the other, C, 38 tests of 8 series each, each series containing 13 syllables. The results obtained were as follows:

1. For the tests at time B: $m = 871$, P.E.$_0 = \pm 63$.

DISTRIBUTION OF THE SEPARATE VALUES

| Within the limits | Number of deviations | |
|---|---|---|
| | Counted | Calculated |
| $\frac{1}{4}$ P.E. | 4 | 5 |
| $\frac{1}{2}$ P.E. | 10 | 10.3 |
| P.E. | 21 | 19.5 |
| $1\frac{1}{2}$ P.E. | 28 | 26.8 |
| 2 P.E. | 32 | 32.0 |
| $2\frac{1}{2}$ P.E. | 35 | 35.4 |
| 3 P.E. | 37 | 37.3 |

2. For the tests of time C: $m = 1{,}258$, P.E.$_0 = \pm 60$.

DISTRIBUTION OF THE SEPARATE VALUES

| Within the limits | Number of deviations | |
|---|---|---|
| | Counted | Calculated |
| $\frac{1}{4}$ P.E. | 7 | 5.0 |
| $\frac{1}{2}$ P.E. | 10 | 10.0 |
| P.E. | 19 | 19.0 |
| $1\frac{1}{2}$ P.E. | 26 | 26.0 |
| 2 P.E. | 31 | 31.0 |
| $2\frac{1}{2}$ P.E. | 34 | 34.5 |
| 3 P.E. | 36 | 36.4 |

In addition I mention a series of only twenty tests, with which I shall conclude this summary. Each test consisted of the learning of eight separate series of thirteen syllables each, which had been memorised once one month before. The average was in this case 892 seconds with a probable error of observation of 54. The single values were grouped as follows:

| Within the limits | Number of deviations | |
|---|---|---|
| | Counted | Calculated |
| $\frac{1}{4}$ P.E. | 3 | 2.7 |
| $\frac{1}{2}$ P.E. | 5 | 5.3 |
| P.E. | 10 | 10.0 |
| $1\frac{1}{2}$ P.E. | 12 | 13.8 |
| 2 P.E. | 17 | 16.5 |
| $2\frac{1}{2}$ P.E. | 19 | 18.2 |
| 3 P.E. | 20 | 19.1 |

Although the number of the tests was so small, the accordance between the calculation by theory and the actual count of deviations is in all these cases so close that the usefulness of the mean values will be admitted, the wide limits of error being, of course, taken into consideration.

### Section 18. Grouping of the Results of the Separate Series

The previously mentioned hypotheses concerning the grouping of the times necessary for learning the separate series were naturally not merely theoretical suppositions, but had already been confirmed by the groupings actually found. The two large series of tests mentioned above, one consisting of 92 tests of eight single series each, and the other of 84 tests of 6 single series each, thus giving 736 and 504 separate values respectively, afford a sufficiently broad basis for judgment. Both groups of numbers, and both in the same way, show the following peculiarities:

1. The distribution of the arithmetical values above their mean is considerably looser and extends farther than below the mean. The most extreme values above lie 2 times and 1.8 times, respectively, as far from the mean as the most distant of those below.

2. As a result of this dominance by the higher numbers the mean is displaced upward from the region of the densest distribution, and as a result the deviations below get the preponderance in number. There occur respectively 404 and 266 deviations below as against 329 and 230 above.

3. The number of deviations from the region of densest distribution towards both limits does not decrease uniformly—as one would be very much inclined to expect from the relatively large numbers combined—but several maxima and minima of density are distinctly noticeable. Therefore constant sources of error were at work in the production of the separate values— i.e., in the memorisation of the separate series. These resulted on the one hand in an unsymmetrical distribution of the numbers, and on the other hand in an accumulation of them in certain regions. In accordance with the investigations already presented in this chapter, it can only be supposed that these influences compensated each other when the values of several series learned in succession were combined.

I have already mentioned as the probable cause of this unsymmetrical distribution the peculiar variations in the effect of high degrees of concentration of attention and distraction. It would naturally be supposed that the position of the separate series within each test is the cause of the repeated piling up of values on each side of the average. If, in the case of a large test-series, the values are summed up for the first, the second, and third series, etc., and the average of each is taken, these average values vary greatly, as might be expected. The separate values are grouped about their mean with only tolerable approximation to the law of error, but yet they are, on the whole, distributed most densely in its region, and these separate regions of dense distribution must of course appear in the total result.

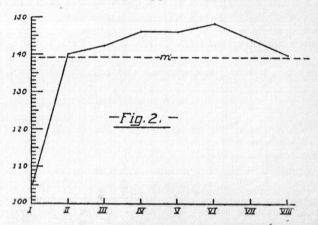

The following may be added by way of supplement: on account of the mental fatigue which increases gradually during the course of a test-series the mean values ought to increase with the number of the series; but this does not prove to be the case.

Only in one case have I been able to notice anything corresponding to this hypothesis, namely, in the large and therefore important series of 92 tests consisting of eight series of 13 syllables each. In this case the mean values for the learning of the 92 first series, the 92 second series, etc., were found to be 105, 140, 142, 146, 146, 148, 144, 140 seconds, the relative lengths of which Fig. 2 exhibits. For all the rest of the cases which I investigated the typical fact is, on the contrary, rather such a course of the numbers as was true in the case of the series of 84 tests of six series of 16 syllables each and as is shown in Fig. 3.

The mean values here were 191, 224, 206, 218, 210, 213 seconds. They start in, as may be seen, considerably below the average, but rise immediately to a height which is not again reached in the further course of the test, and they then oscillate

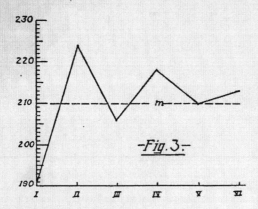

-Fig. 3.-

rather decidedly. An analogous course is shown by the numbers in the 7 tests of nine 12-syllable series, namely: 71, 90, 98, 87, 98, 90, 101, 86, 69 (Fig. 4).

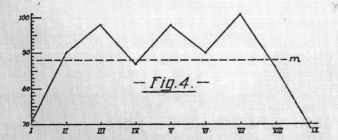

- Fig. 4. -

Furthermore the values for 39 tests of six series of 13 syllables each obtained in time B were as follows: 118, 150, 158, 147, 155, 144 (Fig. 5 lower curve).

Those for 38 tests with eight 13 syllable series of time C were 139, 159, 167, 168, 160, 150, 162, 153 (Fig. 5 upper curve).

Finally the numbers obtained from seven tests with six stanzas of Byron's "Don Juan" were: 189, 219, 171, 204, 183, 229.

Even in the case of the first mentioned contradictory group
of tests a grouping of the separate mean values harmonising with
the normal one occurs if, instead of all the 92 tests being taken
into consideration at once, they are divided into several parts—
*i.e.*, if tests are combined which were taken at about the same
time and under about the same conditions.

The conclusion cannot be drawn from these numerical results
that the mental fatigue which gradually increased during the
twenty minute duration of the tests did not exert any influence.

It can only be said that the supposed influence of the latter
upon the numbers is far outweighed by another tendency which

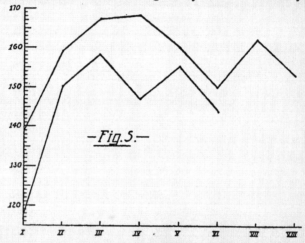

would not *a priori* be so readily suspected, namely the tendency
of comparatively low values to be followed by comparatively high
ones and vice versa. There seems to exist a kind of periodical
oscillation of mental receptivity or attention in connection with
which the increasing fatigue expresses itself by fluctuations
around a median position which is gradually displaced.[1]

[1] If it should ever become a matter of interest, the attempt might be
made to define numerically the different effects of that tendency in different cases. For the probable errors of observation for the numerical
values of series-groups afford a measure for the influence of accidental
disturbances to which the memorisation is daily exposed. If now the
learning of the separate series in general were exposed to the same or
similar variations of condition as occur from test to test, then according
to the fundamental principles of the theory of errors, a probable error of
observation calculated directly from the separate values would relate itself
to the one just mentioned as 1 to $\sqrt{n}$, where "n" denotes the number of
separate series combined into a test. If, however, as is the case here,
special influences assert themselves during the memorisation of these

After orienting ourselves thus concerning the nature and value of the numerical results gained from the complete memorisations, we shall now turn to the real purpose of the investigation, namely the numerical description of causal relations.

separate series, and if such influences tend to separate the values further than other variations of conditions would do, the " P.E.$_0$ " calculated from the separate values must turn out somewhat too great, and the just mentioned proportion consequently too small, and the stronger the influences are, the more must this be the case.

An examination of the actual relations is, to be sure, a little difficult, but fully confirms the statements. In the 84 tests, consisting of six series of 16 syllables each, the $\sqrt{n} = 2.45$. We found 48.4 to be the probable error of observation of the 84 tests. The probable error of the 504 separate values is 31.6. The quotient 31.6 : 48.4 is 1.53; therefore not quite $\frac{2}{3}$ of the value of $\sqrt{n}$.

# CHAPTER V

## RAPIDITY OF LEARNING SERIES OF SYLLABLES AS A FUNCTION OF THEIR LENGTH

### Section 19.   Tests Belonging to the Later Period

It is sufficiently well known that the memorisation of a series of ideas that is to be reproduced at a later time is more difficult, the longer the series is. That is, the memorisation not only requires more time taken by itself, because each repetition lasts longer, but it also requires more time relatively because an increased number of repetitions becomes necessary. Six verses of a poem require for learning not only three times as much time as two but considerably more than that.

I did not investigate especially this relation of dependence, which of course becomes evident also in the first possible reproduction of series of nonsense syllables, but incidentally I obtained a few numerical values for it which are worth putting down, although they do not show particularly interesting relations.

The series in question comprised (in the case of the tests of the year 1883-84), 12, 16, 24, or 36 syllables each, and

9, 6, 3, or 2 series were each time combined into a test.

For the number of repetitions necessary in these cases to memorise the series up to the first errorless reproduction (and including it) the following numerical results were found:

| X series | Y syllables each | Required together an average of Z repetitions | Probable error of average values | Number of tests |
|---|---|---|---|---|
| X= | Y= | Z= | | |
| 9 | 12 | 158 | ± 3.4 | 7 |
| 6 | 16 | 186 | ± 0.9 | 42 |
| 3 | 24 | 134 | ± 2.9 | 7 |
| 2 | 36 | 112 | ± 4.0 | 7 |

In order to make the number of repetitions comparable it is necessary, so to speak, to reduce them to a common denominator and to divide them each time by the number of the series. In this way it is found out how many repetitions relatively were necessary to learn by heart the single series, which differ from each other only in the number of syllables, and which each time had been taken together with as many others of the same kind as would make the duration of the whole test from fifteen to thirty minutes.[1]

However, a conclusion can be drawn from the figures from the standpoint of decrease in number of syllables. The question can be asked: What number of syllables can be correctly recited after only one reading? For me the number is usually seven. Indeed I have often succeeded in reproducing eight syllables, but this has happened only at the beginning of the tests and in a decided minority of the cases. In the case of six syllables on the other hand a mistake almost never occurs; with them, therefore, a single attentive reading involves an unnecessarily large expenditure of energy for an immediately following reproduction.

If this latter pair of values is added, the required division made, and the last faultless reproduction subtracted as not necessary for the learning, then the following table results.

| Number of syllables in a series | Number of repetitions necessary for first errorless reproduction (exclusive of it) | Probable error |
|---|---|---|
| 7 | 1 | |
| 12 | 16.6 | ± 1.1 |
| 16 | 30.0 | ± 0.4 |
| 24 | 44.0 | ± 1.7 |
| 36 | 55.0 | ± 2.8 |

---

[1] The objection might be made that, by means of this division, recourse is made directly to the averages for the memorising of the single series, and that in this way the result of the Fourth Chapter is disregarded. For, according to that, the averages of the numbers obtained from groups of series could indeed be used for investigation into relations of dependence, but the averages obtained from separate series could not be so used. I do not claim, however, that the above numbers, thus obtained by division, form the correct average for the numbers belonging to the separate series, *i.e.*, that the latter group themselves according to the law of errors. But the numbers are to be considered as averages for groups of series, and, for the sake of a better comparison with others—a condition which in the nature of the case could not be everywhere the same—is made the same by division. The probable error, the measure of their accuracy, has not been calculated from the numbers for the separate series but from those for the groups of series.

The longer of the two adjoining curves of Fig. 6 illustrates the regular course of these numbers with approximate accuracy for such a small number of tests. As Fig. 6 shows, in the cases examined, the number of repetitions necessary for the memorisation of series in which the number of syllables progressively increased, itself increases with extraordinary rapidity with the increase in number of the syllables.

At first the ascent of the curve is very steep, but later on it appears to gradually flatten out. For the mastery of five times

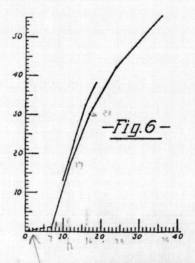

– Fig. 6 –

the number of syllables that can be reproduced after but one reading—*i.e.*, after about 3 seconds—over 50 repetitions were necessary, requiring an uninterrupted and concentrated effort for fifteen minutes.

The curve has its natural starting point in the zero point of the co-ordinates. The short initial stretch up to the point, $x = 7$, $y = 1$, can be explained thus: in order to recite by heart series of 6, 5, 4, etc., syllables one reading, of course, is all that is necessary. In my case this reading does not require as much attention as does the 7-syllable one, but can become more and more superficial as the number of syllables decreases.

### Section 20.  Tests Belonging to the Earlier Period

It goes without saying that since the results reported were obtained from only one person they have meaning only as related to him.  The question arises whether they are for this individual of a general significance—*i.e.*, whether, by repetition of the tests at another time, they could be expected to show approximately the same amount and grouping.

A series of results from the earlier period furnishes the desired possibility of a control in this direction.  They, again, have been obtained incidentally (consequently uninfluenced by expectations and suppositions) and from tests made under different conditions than those mentioned.  These earlier tests occurred at an earlier hour of the day and the learning was continued until the separate series could be recited twice in succession without mistake.  A test comprised

> 15 series of 10 syllables each,
> or 8   "   "  13     "      "
> or 6   "   "  16     "      "
> or 4   "   "  19     "      "

So, again, four different lengths of series have been taken into account, but their separate values lie much closer together.

Since the repetitions—which are in question here—were not counted at all in the earlier period, their number had to be calculated from the times.  For this purpose the table on p. 31 has been used after corresponding interpolation.  If the numbers found are immediately reduced to one series each, and if along with it the two repetitions representing the recitation are subtracted as above, we obtain:

| Number of syllables in a series | Number of repetitions necessary for two errorless reproductions (exclusive of them) | Probable error[1] | Number of tests |
|---|---|---|---|
| 10 | 13 | ± 1. | 16 |
| 13 | 23 | ± 0.5 | 92 |
| 16 | 32 | ± 1.2 | 6 |
| 19 | 38 | ± 2.0 | 11 |

[1] The probable errors are based upon calculation and have only an approximate value.

The smaller curve of Fig. 6 exhibits graphically the arrangement of these numbers. As may be seen, the number of repetitions necessary for learning equally long series was a little larger in the earlier period than in the later one. Because of its uniformity this relation is to be attributed to differences in the experimental conditions, to inaccuracies in the calculations, and perhaps also to the increased training of the later period. The older numbers fall very close to the position of the later ones, and—what is of chief importance—the two curves lie as closely together throughout the short extent of their common course as could be desired for tests separated by 3½ years and unaffected by any presuppositions. There is a high degree of probability, then, in favor of the supposition that the relations of dependence presented in those curves, since they remained constant over a long interval of time, are to be considered as characteristic for the person concerned, although they are, to be sure, only individual.

### Section 21.  *Increase in Rapidity of Learning in the Case of Meaningful Material*

In order to keep in mind the similarities and differences between sense and nonsense material, I occasionally made tests with the English original of Byron's "Don Juan." These results do not properly belong here since I did not vary the length of the amount to be learned each time but memorised on each occasion only separate stanzas. Nevertheless, it is interesting to mention the number of repetitions necessary because of their contrast with the numerical results just given.

There are only seven tests (1884) to be considered, each of which comprised six stanzas. When the latter, each by itself, were learned to the point of the first possible reproduction, an average of 52 repetitions (P.E.$_m = \pm 0.6$) was necessary for all six taken together. Thus, each stanza required hardly nine repetitions; or, if the errorless reproduction is abstracted, scarcely eight repetitions.[1]

---

[1] For the sake of correct evaluation of the numbers and correct connection with possible individual observations, please note p. 24, 1. In order to procure uniformity of method the stanzas were always read through from beginning to end; more difficult passages were not learned separately and then inserted. If that had been done, the times would have been much shorter and nothing could have been said about

If it is born in mind that each stanza contains 80 syllables (each syllable, however, consisting on the average of less than three letters) and if the number of repetitions here found is compared with the results presented above, there is obtained an approximate numerical expression for the extraordinary advantage which the combined ties of meaning, rhythm, rhyme, and a common language give to material to be memorised. If the above curve is projected in imagination still further along its present course, then it must be supposed that I would have required 70 to 80 repetitions for the memorisation of a series of 80 to 90 nonsense syllables. When the syllables were objectively and subjectively united by the ties just mentioned this requirement was in my case reduced to about one-tenth of that amount.

---

the number of repetitions. Of course the reading was done at a uniform rate of speed as far as possible, but not in the slow and mechanically regulated time that was employed for the series of syllables. The regulation of speed was left to free estimation. A single reading of one stanza required 20 to 23 seconds.

# CHAPTER VI

## RETENTION AS A FUNCTION OF THE NUMBER OF REPETITIONS

### *Section 22. Statement of the Problem*

The result of the fourth chapter was as follows: When in repeated cases I memorised series of syllables of a certain length to the point of their first possible reproduction, the times (or number of repetitions) necessary differed greatly from each other, but the mean values derived from them had the character of genuine constants of natural science. Ordinarily, therefore, I learned by heart homogeneous series under similar conditions with, on the average, a similar number of repetitions. The large deviations of the separate values from each other change the total result not at all; but it would require too much time to ascertain with exactness the number necessary for greater precision in detail.

What will happen, it may be asked, if the number of repetitions actually given to a certain series is less than is required for memorisation or if the number exceeds the necessary minimum?

The general nature of what happens has already been described. Naturally the surplus repetitions of the latter alternative do not go to waste. Even though the immediate effect, the smooth and errorless reproduction, is not affected by them, yet they are not without significance in that they serve to make other such reproductions possible at a more or less distant time. The longer a person studies, the longer he retains. And, even in the first case, something evidently occurs even if the repetitions do not suffice for a free reproduction. By them a way is at least opened for the first errorless reproduction, and the disconnected, hesitating, and faulty reproductions keep approximating more and more to it.

These relations can be described figuratively by speaking of the

52

series as being more or less deeply engraved in some mental substratum. To carry out this figure: as the number of repetitions increases, the series are engraved more and more deeply and indelibly; if the number of repetitions is small, the inscription is but surface deep and only fleeting glimpses of the tracery can be caught; with a somewhat greater number the inscription can, for a time at least, be read at will; as the number of repetitions is still further increased, the deeply cut picture of the series fades out only after ever longer intervals.

What is to be said in case a person is not satisfied with this general statement of a relation of dependence between the number of repetitions and the depth of the mental impression obtained, and if he demands that it be defined more clearly and in detail? The thermometer rises with increasing temperature, the magnetic needle is displaced to an increasing angle as the intensity of the electric current around it increases. But while the mercury always rises by equal spaces for each equal increase in temperature, the increase of the angle showing the displacement of the magnetic needle becomes less with a like increase in the electric current. Which analogy is it which holds for the effect of the number of repetitions of the series to be memorised upon the depth of the resulting impression? Without further discussion shall we make it proportional to the number of repetitions, and accordingly say that it is twice or three times as great when homogenous series are repeated with the same degree of attention twice or thrice as many times as are others? Or does it increase less and less with each and every constant increase in the number of repetitions? Or what does happen?

Evidently this question is a good one; its answer would be of theoretical as well as practical interest and importance. But with the resources hitherto at hand it could not be answered, nor even investigated. Even its meaning will not be quite clear so long as the words " inner stability " and " depth of impression " denote something indefinite and figurative rather than something clear and objectively defined.

Applying the principles developed in section 5, I define the inner stability of a series of ideas—the degree of its retainability —by the greater or less readiness with which it is reproduced at some definite time subsequent to its first memorisation. This readiness I measure by the amount of work saved in the re-

learning of any series as compared with the work necessary
for memorising a similar but entirely new series.

The interval of time between the two processes of memorisation is of course a matter of choice. I chose 24 hours.

Since in the case of this definition we are not trying to settle
a matter of general linguistic usage, it cannot be properly asked
whether it is correct, but only whether it serves the purpose,
or, at the most, whether it is applicable to the indefinite ideas
connected with the notion of different depths of mental impression. The latter will probably be granted. But nothing can
be said in advance as to how well it fulfills its purpose. That
can be judged only after more extensive results have been obtained. And the character of the judgment will depend to a
great extent on whether the results obtained with the help of
this means of measurement fulfill the primary demand which
we make with reference to any system of measurement. It
consists in this,—that if any change whatever is made in the
controllable conditions of that scale, the results obtained
by the scale in its new form can be reduced to those of the old
form by multiplication by some one constant. In our present
case, for example, it would consequently be necessary to know
whether the *character* of the results would remain the same if
any other interval had been employed instead of that of 24 hours,
arbitrarily chosen for measuring the after-effect of repetitions,
or whether as a consequence the entire rationale of the results
would be different, just as the absolute values are necessarily
different. Naturally, this question cannot be decided *a priori*.

For ascertaining the relation of dependence between the increase in the number of repetitions of a series and the ever
deeper impression of it which results, I have formulated the
problem as follows: If homogeneous series are impressed to
different extents as a result of different numbers of repetitions,
and then 24 hours later are learned to the point of the first
possible reproduction by heart, how are the resulting savings in
work related to each other and to the corresponding number of
former repetitions?

## Section 23. The Tests and their Results

In order to answer the question just formulated, I have carried out 70 double tests, each of six series of 16 syllables each.

Each double test consisted in this, that the separate series—each for itself—were first read attentively a given number of times (after frequently repeated readings they were recited by heart instead of read), and that 24 hours later I relearned up to the point of first possible reproduction the series thus impressed and then in part forgotten. The first reading was repeated 8, 16, 24, 32, 42, 53, or 64 times.

An increase of the readings used for the first learning beyond 64 repetitions proved impracticable, at least for six series of this length. For with this number each test requires about ¾ of an hour, and toward the end of this time exhaustion, headache, and other symptoms were often felt which would have complicated the conditions of the test if the number of repetitions had been increased.

The tests were equally divided among the seven numbers of repetitions investigated so that to each of them were allotted 10 double tests. The results were as follows for the six series of a single test taken together and without subtraction of the time used for reciting.

After a preceding study of the series by means of " x " repetitions, they were learned 24 hours later with an expenditure of " y " seconds.

| x = 8 y = | x = 16 y = | x = 24 y = | x = 32 y = | x = 42 y = | x = 53 y = | x = 64 y = |
|---|---|---|---|---|---|---|
| 1171 | 998 | 1013 | 736 | 708 | 615 | 530 |
| 1070 | 795 | 853 | 764 | 579 | 579 | 483 |
| 1204 | 936 | 854 | 863 | 734 | 601 | 499 |
| 1180 | 1124 | 908 | 850 | 660 | 561 | 464 |
| 1246 | 1168 | 1004 | 892 | 738 | 618 | 412 |
| 1113 | 1160 | 1068 | 868 | 713 | 582 | 419 |
| 1283 | 1189 | 979 | 913 | 649 | 572 | 417 |
| 1141 | 1186 | 966 | 858 | 634 | 516 | 397 |
| 1127 | 1164 | 1076 | 914 | 788 | 550 | 391 |
| 1139 | 1059 | 1033 | 975 | 763 | 660 | 524 |

$m$ = 1167, 1078, 975, 863, 697, 585, 454
$P.E._m$ = ±14, ± 28, ± 17, ± 15, ± 14, ± 9, ± 11

The preceding table of numbers gives the times *actually used* in learning by heart the series studied 24 hours previously. Since we are interested not so much in the times used as the times saved, we must know how long it would have taken to learn by heart the same series if no previous study had been made. In the case of the series which were repeated 42, 53, and 64 times,

this time can be learned from the tests themselves. For, in
their case, the number of repetitions is greater than the average
minimum for the first possible reproduction, which in the case
of the 16-syllable series (p. 46) amounted to 31 repetitions. In their case, therefore, the point can be determined
at which the first errorless reproduction of that series appeared
as the number of repetitions kept on increasing. But on account
of the continued increase in the number of repetitions and the
resulting extension of the time of the test, the conditions were
somewhat different from those in the customary learning of
series not hitherto studied. In the case of the series to which
a smaller number of repetitions than the above were given, the
numbers necessary for comparison cannot be derived from their
own records, since, as a part of the plan of the experiment, they
were not completely learned by heart. I have consequently pre-
ferred each time to find the saving of work in question by comparison with the time required for learning by heart not the
same but a similar series up to that time unknown. For this
I possess a fairly correct numerical value from the time of the
tests in question: any six 16-syllable series was learned, as an
average of 53 tests, in 1,270 seconds, with the small probable
error ± 7.

If all the mean values are brought together in relation to this
last value, the following table results:

| I After a preceding study of the series by X repetitions, | II They were just memorized 24 hours later in Y seconds | | III The result therefore of the preceding study was a saving of T seconds, | | IV Or, for each of the repetitions, an average saving of D seconds |
|---|---|---|---|---|---|
| X= | Y= | $P.E._m$= | T= | $P.E._m$= | D= |
| 0 | 1270 | 7 | | | |
| 8 | 1167 | 14 | 103 | 16 | 12.9 |
| 16 | 1078 | 28 | 192 | 29 | 12.0 |
| 24 | 975 | 17 | 295 | 19 | 12.3 |
| 32 | 863 | 15 | 407 | 17 | 12.7 |
| 42 | 697 | 14 | 573 | 16 | 13.6 |
| 53 | 585 | 9 | 685 | 11 | 12.9 |
| 64 | 454 | 11 | 816 | 13 | 12.8 |
| | | | | | $m$= 12.7 |

The simple relation approximately realised in these numbers is evident: the number of repetitions used to impress the series (Column I) and the saving in work in learning the series 24 hours later as a result of such impression (Col. III) increase in the same fashion. Division of the amount of work saved by the corresponding number of repetitions gives as a quotient a practically constant value (Col. IV).

Consequently the results of the test may be summarised and formulated as follows: When nonsense series of 16 syllables each were impressed in memory to greater and greater degrees by means of attentive repetitions, the inner depth of impression in part resulting from the number of the repetitions increased, within certain limits, approximately proportionally to that number. This increase in depth was measured by the greater readiness with which these series were brought to the point of reproduction after 24 hours. The limits within which this relation was determined were on the one side, zero, and, on the other, about double the number of repetitions that on the average just sufficed for learning the series.

For six series taken together the after-effect of each repetition—*i.e.*, the saving it brought about—amounted on the average to 12.7 seconds, consequently to 2.1 seconds for each single series. As the repetition of a series of 16 syllables in itself takes from 6.6 to 6.8 seconds, its after-effect 24 hours later amounts to a scant third of its own duration. In other words: for each three additional repetitions which I spent on a given day on the study of a series, I saved, in learning that series 24 hours later, on the average, approximately one repetition; and, within the limits stated, it did not matter how many repetitions altogether were spent on the memorisation of a series.

Whether the results found can claim any more general importance, or whether they hold good only for the single time of their actual occurrence, and even then give a false impression of a regularity not otherwise present, I cannot now decide. I have no direct control tests. Later, however, (chapter VIII, § 34) where results obtained in reference to quite a different problem agree with the present results, I can bring forward indirect evidence on this point. I am therefore inclined to ascribe general validity to these results, at least for my own case.

NOTE.—There is in the tests an inner inequality which I can neither avoid, nor remove by correction, but can only point out. It is that a small number of repetitions of the series requires only a few minutes, and consequently come at a time of unusual mental vitality. With 64 repetitions the whole work takes about ¾ of an hour; the great part of the series is, therefore, studied in a condition of diminished vigor or even of a certain exhaustion, and the repetitions will, consequently, be less effective. It is just the reverse of this in the reproduction of the series the next day. The series impressed by 8 perusals require three times as much time in order to be memorised as those perused 64 times. Consequently the latter will be learned a little more quickly not only on account of their greater fixedness, but also because they are now studied for the most part under better conditions. These irregularities are mutually opposed, as is evident, and therefore partially compensate each other: the series prepared under comparatively unfavorable conditions are memorised under comparatively more favorable conditions, and vice versa. I cannot tell, however, how far this compensation goes and how far any remaining inequality of conditions disturbs the results.

### Section 24. The Influence of Recollection

One factor in the regular course of the results obtained seems to deserve special attention. In ordinary life it is of the greatest importance, as far as the form which memory assumes is concerned, whether the reproductions occur with accompanying recollection or not,—*i.e.*, whether the recurring ideas simply return or whether a knowledge of their former existence and circumstances comes back with them. For, in this second case, they obtain a higher and special value for our practical aims and for the manifestations of higher mental life. The question now is, what connection is there between the inner life of these ideas and the complicated phenomena of recollection which sometimes do and sometimes do not accompany the appearance in consciousness of images? Our results contribute somewhat toward the answer to this question.

When the series were repeated 8 or 16 times they had become unfamiliar to me by the next day. Of course, indirectly, I knew quite well that they must be the same as the ones studied the day before, but I knew this only indirectly. I did not get it from the series, I did not recognise them. But with 53 or 64 repetitions I soon, if not immediately, treated them as old acquaintances, I remembered them distinctly. Nothing corresponding to this difference is evident in the times for memorisation and for savings of work respectively. They are not smaller *relatively* when there is no possibility of recollection nor larger *relatively* when recollection is sure and vivid. The regularity of the after-effect of many repetitions does not noticeably deviate from the line that is, so to speak, marked out by a smaller number of repetitions although the occurrence of this after-effect is accompanied by recollection in the first case just as indubitably as it lacks recollection in the second case.

I restrict myself to pointing out this noteworthy fact. General conclusions from it would lack foundation as long as the common cause cannot be proved.

## Section 25. The Effect of a Decided Increase in the Number of Repetitions

It would be of interest to know whether the approximate proportionality between the number of repetitions of a series and the saving of the work in relearning the latter made possible thereby, which in my own case seemed to take place within certain limits, continues to exist beyond those limits. If, furthermore, as a result of each repetition a scant third of its own value is saved up to be applied on the reproduction 24 hours later, I should be able to just reproduce spontaneously after 24 hours a series of 16 syllables, the initial syllable being given, provided I had repeated it the first day thrice as many times as were absolutely necessary for its first reproduction. As this requirement is 31-32 repetitions the attainment of the aim in question would necessitate about 100 repetitions. On the supposition of the general validity of the relation found, the number of repetitions to be made at a given time, in order that errorless reproduction might take place 24 hours later, could be calculated for any kind of series for which, so to say, the " after-effect-coefficient " of the repetitions had been ascertained.

I have not investigated this question by further increasing the number of repetitions of unfamiliar 16 syllable series because, as has been already noted, with any great extension of the tests the increasing fatigue and a certain drowsiness cause complications. However, I have made some trial tests partly with shorter series, and partly with familiar series, all of which confirmed the result that the proportion in question gradually ceases to hold with a further increase of repetitions. Measured by the saving of work after 24 hours the effect of the later repetitions gradually decreases.

Series of 12 syllables (six of the series were each time combined into a test) were studied to the point of first possible reproduction; and immediately after the errorless reproduction each series was repeated three times (in all four times) as often as the memorisation (exclusive of the recital) had required. After 24 hours the same series were relearned to the first possible reproduction. Four tests furnished the following results (the numbers indicate the repetitions):

| Repetitions for the learning and recital of 6 series | Immediately successive repetitions for the sake of greater surety | Total number of repetitions used for the 6 series | After 24 hours the memorization of the series required | Thus the work saved by the total number of repetitions amounted to |
|---|---|---|---|---|
| 104 | 294 | 398 | 41 | 63 |
| 101 | 285 | 386 | 39 | 62 |
| 114 | 324 | 438 | 46 | 68 |
| 109 | 309 | .418 | 38 | 71 |
| $m=$ 107 | 303 | 410 | 41 | 66 $P.E._m = 1.4$ |

In my own case—within reasonable limits—the after-effect of the repetitions of series of 12 syllables after 24 hours is a little smaller than is the case with 16 syllables; it must be estimated as at least three tenths of the sum total of the repetitions. If this relation were approximately to continue to hold with very numerous repetitions, it would be reasonable to expect that, after 24 hours, series on whose impression four times as many repetitions had been expended as were necessary for their first reproduction could be recited without any further expenditure of energy. Instead of this, in the cases examined, the relearning required about 35 per cent of the work required for the first recital. The effect of an average number of 410 repetitions was a saving of only one sixth of this sum. If now the first repetitions were represented by about three tenths of their amount, the effect of the later repetitions must have been very slight.

Investigations of the following kind, which I do not here give in detail, led to the same result. Syllable series of different lengths were gradually memorised by frequent repetitions which, however, did not all take place on one day, but were distributed over several successive days (Chap. VIII). When, after several days, only a few repetitions were necessary in order to learn the series by heart, they were repeated three or four times as often as was necessary, at this phase of memorisation, for the first errorless reproduction. But in no single case did I succeed in an errorless reproduction of the series after 24 hours unless I had read them again once or several times. The influence of the frequent repetitions still appeared, indeed, in a certain saving of work, but this became less in proportion to the decreasing amount of work to be saved. It was very hard, by means of repetitions which had taken place 24 hours previously, to eliminate the last remnant of the work of relearning a given series.

To summarise: The effect of increasing the number of repetitions of series of syllables on their inner fixedness in the above defined sense grew at first approximately in proportion to the number of repetitions, then that effect decreased gradually, and finally became very slight when the series were so deeply impressed that they could be repeated after 24 hours, almost spontaneously. Since this decrease must be considered gradual and continuous, its beginning would, in more accurate investigations, probably have become evident even within the limits within which we found a proportionality, whereas now it is hidden on account of its small amount and the wide limits of error.

# CHAPTER VII

## RETENTION AND OBLIVISCENCE AS A FUNCTION OF THE TIME

### Section 26. *Explanations of Retention and Obliviscence*

All sorts of ideas, if left to themselves, are gradually forgotten. This fact is generally known. Groups or series of ideas which at first we could easily recollect or which recurred frequently of their own accord and in lively colors, gradually return more rarely and in paler colors, and can be reproduced by voluntary effort only with difficulty and in part. After a longer period even this fails, except, to be sure, in rare instances. Names, faces, bits of knowledge and experience that had seemed lost for years suddenly appear before the mind, especially in dreams, with every detail present and in great vividness; and it is hard to see whence they came and how they managed to keep hidden so well in the meantime. Psychologists—each in accordance with his general standpoint—interpret these facts from different points of view, which do not exclude each other entirely but still do not quite harmonise. One set, it seems, lays most importance on the remarkable recurrence of vivid images even after long periods. They suppose that of the perceptions caused by external impressions there remain pale images, "traces," which, although in every respect weaker and more flighty than the original perceptions, continue to exist unchanged in the intensity possessed at present. These mental images cannot compete with the much more intense and compact perceptions of real life; but where the latter are missing entirely or partly, the former domineer all the more unrestrainedly. It is also true that the earlier images are more and more overlaid, so to speak, and covered by the later ones. Therefore, in the case of the earlier images, the possibility of recurrence offers itself more rarely and with greater difficulty. But if, by an accidental and favorable grouping of circumstances, the accumu-

62

lated layers are pushed to one side, then, of course, that which
was hidden beneath must appear, after whatever lapse of time,
in its original and still existent vividness.[1]

For others[2] the ideas, the persisting images, suffer changes
which more and more affect their nature; the concept of obscuration comes in here.  Older ideas are repressed and forced to sink
down, so to speak, by the more recent ones.  As time passes one
of these general qualities, inner clearness and intensity of consciousness, suffers damage.  Connections of ideas and series of
ideas are subject to the same process of progressive weakening;
it is furthered by a resolution of the ideas into their components,
as a result of which the now but loosely connected members are
eventually united in new combinations.  The complete disappearance of the more and more repressed ideas occurs only
after a long time.  But one should not imagine the repressed
ideas in their time of obscuration to be pale images, but rather
to be tendencies, "dispositions," to recreate the image contents
forced to sink down.  If these dispositions are somehow sup-
ported and strengthened, it may happen at any one moment that

---

[1] This is the opinion of Aristotle and is still authoritative for many
people.  Lately, for instance, Delboeuf has taken it up again, and has
used it as a complement to his "théorie générale de la sensibilité."  In
his article, *Le sommeil et les rêves* (*Rev. Philos.* IX, p. 153 f.), he says:
"Nous voyons maintenant que tout acte de sentiment, de pensée ou de
volition en vertu d'une loi universelle imprime en nous une trace plus
ou moins profonde, mais indélébile, généralement gravée sur une infinité
de traits antérieurs, surchargée plus tard d'une autre infinité de linéa-
ments de toute nature, mais dont l'écriture est néanmoins indéfiniment
susceptible de reparaître vive et nette au jour."  (We see now that by
a general law every act of feeling, thought or will leaves a more or less
deep but indelible impress upon our mind, that such a tracing is usually
graven upon an infinite number of previous traces and later is itself overlaid with innumerable others but nevertheless is still capable of vivid
and clear reappearance.)  It is true that he proceeds: "néanmoins   . . .
il y a quelque vérité dans l'opinion qui veut que la mémoire non seulement
se fatigue mais s'oblitère" (nevertheless  . . .  there is some truth
in the opinion that memory not only becomes fatigued but that it disappears"), but he explains this by the theory that one memory might
hinder another from appearing.  "Si un souvenir ne chasse pas l'autre
on peut du moins prétendre qu'un souvenir empêche l'autre et qu'ainsi
pour la substance cérébrale, chez l'individu, il y a un maximum de
saturation."  (If one recollection does not actually drive out another,
it may at least be maintained that one recollection hinders the other and
that thus the brain of each individual is saturated.)
The curious theory of Bain and others that each idea is lodged in
a separate ganglion cell, an hypothesis impossible both psychologically
and physiologically, is also rooted to a certain extent in Aristotle's view.
[2] Herbart and his adherents.  See, for instance, Waitz, Lehrbuch der
Psychologie Sect. 16.

the repressing and hindering ideas become depressed themselves, and that the apparently forgotten idea arises again in perfect clearness.

A third view holds that, at least in the case of complex ideas, obliviscence consists in the crumbling into parts and the loss of separate components instead of in general obscuration. The idea of resolution into component parts recently spoken of supplies here the only explanation. " The image of a complex object is dim in our memory not because as a whole with all its parts present and in order it is illuminated by a feebler light of consciousness, but it is because it has become incomplete. Some parts of it are entirely lacking. Above all the precise connection of those still extant is, in general, missing and is supplied only by the thought that some sort of union once existed between them; the largeness of the sphere in which, without being able to make a final decision, we think this or that connection equally probable, determines the degree of dimness which we are to ascribe to the idea in question."[1]

Each of these opinions receives a certain, but not exclusive, support from the actual inner experiences, or experiences supposed to be actual, which we at times have. And what is the reason? It is that these fortuitous and easily obtained inner experiences are much too vague, superficial and capable of various interpretations to admit in their entirety of only a single interpretation, or even to let it appear as of preponderating probability. Who could, with even tolerable exactness, describe in its gradual course the supposed overlaying or sinking or crumbling of ideas? Who can say anything satisfactory about the inhibitions caused by series of ideas of different extent, or about the disintegration that a firm complex of any kind suffers by the use of its components in new connections? Everybody has his private " explanation " of these processes, but the actual conditions which are to be explained are, after all, equally unknown to all of us.

If one considers the limitation to direct, unaided observation and to the chance occurrence of useful experiences, there seems but little prospect of improvement in conditions. How will one for example determine the degree of obscuration reached at a certain point, or the number of fragments remaining? Or

---

[1] Lotze, Metaphysik (1879), p. 521; also Mikrokosmos (3) I, p. 231 ff.

how can the probable course of inner processes be traced if
the almost entirely forgotten ideas return no more to consciousness?

### Section 27.  Methods of Investigation of Actual Conditions

By the help of our method we have a possibility of indirectly
approaching the problem just stated in a small and definitely
limited sphere, and, by means of keeping aloof for a while from
any theory, perhaps of constructing one.

After a definite time, the hidden but yet existent dispositions
laid down by the learning of a syllable-series may be strengthened
by a further memorisation of the series, and thereby the remaining fragments may be united again to a whole.  The work necessary for this compared with that necessary when such dispositions and fragments are absent gives a measure for what has
been lost as well as for what remains.  The inhibitions which
idea-groups of different sorts or extents may occasion in relation to others must, as a result of the interposition of well defined
complexes of ideas between learning and relearning, betray itself
in the more or less increased work of relearning.  The loosening
of a bond of connection by some other use of its components
can be investigated in a similar manner as follows: after a certain
series has been studied, new combinations of the same series
are memorised and the change in the amount of work necessary
for relearning the original combination is then ascertained.

First, I investigated the first mentioned of these relations and
put the question: If syllable series of a definite kind are learned
by heart and then left to themselves, how will the process of
forgetting go on when left merely to the influence of time or the
daily events of life which fill it?  The determination of the losses
suffered was made in the way described: after certain intervals
of time, the series memorised were relearned, and the times
necessary in both cases were compared.

The investigations in question fell in the year 1879-80 and
comprised 163 double tests.  Each double test consisted in learning eight series of 13 syllables each (with the exception of 38
double tests taken from 11-12 A. M. which contained only six
series each) and then in relearning them after a definite time.
The learning was continued until two errorless recitations of the
series in question were possible.  The relearning was carried
to the same point; it occurred at one of the following seven

times,—namely, after about one third of an hour, after 1 hour, after 9 hours, one day, two days, six days, or 31 days.

The times were measured from the completion of the first set of first learnings, as a consequence of which no great accuracy was required in case of the longer intervals. The influence of the last four intervals was tested at three different times of day (p. 33). Some preliminary remarks are necessary before the results obtained can be communicated.

Similar experimental conditions may be taken for granted in the case of the series relearned after a number of whole days. At any rate there is no way of meeting the actual fluctuations even when external conditions are as far as possible similar, other than by a multiplication of the tests. Where the inner dissimilarity was presumably the greatest, namely after the interval of an entire month, I approximately doubled the number of tests.

In the case of an interval of nine hours and an interval of one hour between learning and relearning, there existed, however, a noticeably constant difference in the experimental conditions. In the later hours of the day mental vigor and receptivity are less. The series learned in the morning and then relearned at a later hour, aside from other influences, require more work for relearning than they would if the relearning were done at a time of mental vigor equal to that of the original learning. Therefore, in order to become comparable, the numerical values found for relearning must suffer a diminution which, at least in the case of the 8 hour interval, is so considerable that it cannot be neglected. It must be ascertained how much longer it takes to learn at the time of day, B, series which were learned in " a " seconds at the time of day, A. The actual determination of this quantity presupposes more tests than I, up to the present, possess. If a necessary but inexact correction is applied to the numbers found for 1 and for 8 hours, these become even more unreliable than if left to themselves.

In the case of the smallest interval, one third of an hour, the same drawback reappears, though to a less degree; but it is probably compensated for by another circumstance. The interval as a whole is so short that the relearning of the first series of a test followed almost immediately or after an interval of one or two minutes upon the learning of the last series of the same test. For this reason the whole formed, so to speak, one continuous test in which the relearning of the series took place under increasingly unfavorable conditions as regards mental freshness. But on the other hand the relearning after such a short interval was done rather quickly. It took hardly half of the time required for the learning. By this means the interval between the learning and relearning of a certain series became gradually smaller. The later series therefore had more favorable conditions with regard to the time interval. In view of the difficulty of more accurate determinations, I have taken it for granted that these two supposed counteracting influences approximately compensated each other.

### *Section 28. Results*

In the following table I denote by:

L the time of first learning of the series in seconds, just as they were found, therefore including the time for the two recitations.

WL the time for relearning the series also including the recitations.

WLk the time of relearning reduced where necessary by a correction.

⊿ the difference L—WL or L—WLk, as the case may be—that is, the saving of work in the case of relearning.

Q the relation of this saving of work to the time necessary for the first learning, given as a per cent. In the calculation of this quotient I considered only the actual learning time, the time for recitation having been subtracted.[1]

The latter was estimated as being 85 seconds for two recitations of 8 series of 13 syllables each; that would correspond to

[1] A theoretically correct determination of the Probable Errors of the differences and quotients found would be very difficult and troublesome. The directly observed values L and WL would have to be made the basis of it. But the ordinary rules of the theory of errors cannot be applied to these values, because these rules are valid only for observations gained independently of one another, whereas L and WL are inwardly connected because they were obtained from the same series. The source of error, "difficulty of the series," does not vary by chance, but in the same way for each pair of values. Therefore I took here the learning and relearning of the series as a single test and the resulting ⊿ or Q, as the case may be, as its numerical representative. From the independently calculated ⊿ and Q, the probable errors were then calculated just as from directly observed values. That is sufficient for an approximate estimate of the reliability of the numbers.

a duration of 0.41 seconds for each syllable (p. 31).

$$\text{Thus } Q = \frac{100 \, \Delta}{L-85}$$

Finally A, B, C mean the previously mentioned times of day,
10-11 A. M., 11-12 A. M., 6-8 P. M.

I. 19 minutes. 12 tests. Learning and relearning at the time A.

| L | WL | Δ | Q |
|---|---|---|---|
| 1156 | 467 | 689 | 64.3 |
| 1089 | 528 | 561 | 55.9 |
| 1022 | 492 | 530 | 56.6 |
| 1146 | 483 | 663 | 62.5 |
| 1115. | 490 | 625 | 60.7 |
| 1066 | 447 | 619 | 63.1 |
| 985 | 453 | 532 | 59.1 |
| 1066 | 517 | 549 | 56.0 |
| 1364 | 540 | 824 | 64.4 |
| 975 | 577 | 398 | 44.7 |
| 1039 | 528 | 511 | 53.6 |
| 952 | 452 | 500 | 57.7 |
| $m$=1081 | 498 | 583 | 58.2 P.E.$_m$=1 |

II. 63 minutes. 16 tests. The learning at the time A, the relearning
at the time B. For ascertaining the influence of this difference in the time
of day I have the following data. Six series of 13 syllables each were learned
at the time B (not including the time of recitation) in 807 seconds (P.E.$_m$=10)
as an average of 39 tests. Just as many series of the same kind were learned
at the time A in 763 seconds (P.E.$_m$=7) as an average of 92 tests. Thus the
values found in the later period are about 5 per cent. of their own amount
too large as compared with those obtained in the earlier period. Therefore
the times found for relearning at the time B must be decreased by about
5 per cent. to make them comparable with those of learning.

| L | WL | WLk | Δ | Q |
|---|---|---|---|---|
| 1095 | 625 | 594 | 501 | 49.6 |
| 1195 | 821 | 780 | 415 | 37.4 |
| 1133 | 669 | 636 | 497 | 47.4 |
| 1153 | 687 | 653 | 500 | 46.8 |
| 1134 | 626 | 595 | 539 | 51.4 |
| 1075 | 620 | 589 | 486 | 49.1 |
| 1138 | 704 | 669 | 469 | 44.5 |
| 1078 | 565 | 537 | 541 | 54.5 |
| 1205 | 770 | 731 | 474 | 42.3 |
| 1104 | 723 | 687 | 417 | 40.9 |
| 886 | 644 | 612 | 274 | 34.2 |
| 958 | 591 | 562 | 396 | 45.4 |
| 1046 | 739 | 702 | 344 | 35.8 |
| 1122 | 790 | 750 | 372 | 35.9 |
| 1100 | 609 | 579 | 521 | 51.3 |
| 1269 | 709 | 674 | 595 | 50.0 |
| $m$  1106 | 681 | 647 | 459 | 44.2 P.E.$_m$=1 |

III. 525 minutes. 12 tests. The learning at the time A, the relearning at the time C. The different influence of the two times of day is calculated as follows: eight series of 13 syllables each required, with 38 tests at time C, 1173 seconds (P.E.$_m$=10); similar series with 92 tests at time A required 1027 seconds (P.E.$_m$=8). The first number is approximately 12 per cent. of its own value larger than the second; therefore I have subtracted that much from the numerical values found for the time C.

| | L | WL | WLk | $\varDelta$ | Q |
|---|---|---|---|---|---|
| | 1219 | 921 | 811 | 408 | 36.0 |
| | 975 | 815 | 717 | 258 | 29.0 |
| | 1015 | 858 | 755 | 260 | 28.0 |
| | 954 | 784 | 690 | 264 | 30.4 |
| | 1340 | 955 | 840 | 500 | 39.8 |
| | 1061 | 811 | 714 | 347 | 35.6 |
| | 1252 | 784 | 690 | 562 | 48.2 |
| | 1067 | 860 | 757 | 310 | 31.6 |
| | 1343 | 1019 | 897 | 446 | 35.5 |
| | 1181 | 842 | 741 | 440 | 40.1 |
| | 1080 | 799 | 703 | 377 | 37.9 |
| | 1091 | 806 | 709 | 382 | 38.0 |
| $m$ | 1132 | 855 | 752 | 380 | 35.8 P.E.$_m$=1 |

IV. One day. 26 tests, of which 10 were at time A, 8 at time B (here as everywhere consisting of only 6 series each), 8 at time C.

A

| | L | WL | $\varDelta$ | Q |
|---|---|---|---|---|
| | 1072 | 811 | 261 | 26.4 |
| | 1369 | 861 | 508 | 39.6 |
| | 1227 | 823 | 404 | 35.4 |
| | 1263 | 793 | 470 | 39.9 |
| | 1113 | 754 | 359 | 34.9 |
| | 1000 | 644 | 356 | 38.9 |
| | 1103 | 628 | 475 | 46.7 |
| | 888 | 754 | 134 | 16.7 |
| | 1030 | 829 | 201 | 21.3 |
| | 1021 | 660 | 361 | 38.6 |
| $m$ | 1109 | 756 | 353 | 33.8 P.E.$_m$=2 |

B

| L | WL | Δ | Q |
|---|---|---|---|
| 889 | 650 | 239 | 29.0 |
| 824 | 537 | 287 | 37.8 |
| 897 | 593 | 304 | 36.5 |
| 825 | 599 | 226 | 29.7 |
| 854 | 562 | 292 | 37.0 |
| 863 | 761 | 122 | 14.9 |
| 742 | 433 | 309 | 45.6 |
| 907 | 653 | 254 | 30.1 |
| *m* 853 | 599 | 254 | 32.6 |
| | | | P.E.$_m$=2.2 |

C

| L | WL | Δ | Q |
|---|---|---|---|
| 1212 | 935 | 277 | 24.6 |
| 1215 | 797 | 418 | 37.0 |
| 1096 | 647 | 449 | 44.4 |
| 1191 | 684 | 507 | 45.8 |
| 1256 | 898 | 358 | 30.6 |
| 1295 | 781 | 514 | 42.5 |
| 1146 | 936 | 210 | 19.8 |
| 1064 | 750 | 314 | 32.1 |
| *m* 1184 | 803 | 381 | 34.6 |
| | | | P.E.$_m$=2.3 |

The average differences between times of learning and relearning at the different times of day vary somewhat with regard to their absolute values. (Of course in the case of B the number 254 must first be multiplied by 4/3, because it is derived from only 6 series.)  But the relations of these differences to the times of first learning (the Q's) harmonize sufficiently well. If, therefore, all the Q's are combined in a general average, Q=33.7 (P.E.$_m$=1.2).

V. Two days.   26 tests; 11 of these at the time A, 7 at B, 8 at C.

A

| L | WL | Δ | Q |
|---|---|---|---|
| 1066 | 895 | 171 | 17.4 |
| 1314 | 912 | 402 | 32.7 |
| 963 | 855 | 108 | 12.3 |
| 964 | 710 | 254 | 28.9 |
| 1242 | 888 | 354 | 30.6 |
| 1243 | 710 | 533 | 46.0 |
| 1144 | 895 | 249 | 23.5 |
| 1143 | 874 | 269 | 25.4 |
| 1149 | 953 | 196 | 18.4 |
| 1090 | 855 | 235 | 23.4 |
| 1376 | 847 | 529 | 41.0 |
| m   1154 | 854 | 300 | 27.2 |
| | | | P.E.$_m$=2.3 |

B

| L | WL | Δ | Q |
|---|---|---|---|
| 752 | 549 | 203 | 29.5 |
| 1087 | 740 | 347 | 33.9 |
| 1073 | 620 | 453 | 44.9 |
| 826 | 693 | 133 | 17.5 |
| 905 | 548 | 357 | 42.4 |
| 811 | 763 | 48 | 6.4 |
| 782 | 618 | 164 | 22.8 |
| m   891 | 647 | 244 | 28.2 |
| | | | P.E.$_m$=3.5 |

## C

| L | WL | $\varDelta$ | Q |
|---|---|---|---|
| 1246 | 889 | 357 | 31.6 |
| 1231 | 885 | 346 | 30.2 |
| 1273 | 1039 | 234 | 19.7 |
| 1319 | 925 | 394 | 31.9 |
| 1125 | 971 | 154 | 14.8 |
| 1275 | 891 | 384 | 32.3 |
| 1322 | 857 | 465 | 37.6 |
| 1170 | 880 | 290 | 26.7 |
| $m$   1245 | 917 | 328 | 28.1 |
| | | | P.E.$_m$=1.8 |

The combination of the three average values of Q, which are stated in per cents and lie close to each other, for the 26 tests gives Q=27.8 (P.E.$_m$=1.4)

VI. Six days.  26 tests, 10 at the time A, 8 at B, 8 at C.

## A

| L | WL | $\varDelta$ | Q |
|---|---|---|---|
| 1076 | 868 | 208 | 21.0 |
| 992 | 710 | 282 | 31.1 |
| 1082 | 756 | 326 | 32.7 |
| 1260 | 973 | 287 | 24.4 |
| 1032 | 864 | 168 | 17.7 |
| 1010 | 955 | 55 | 5.9 |
| 1197 | 818 | 379 | 34.1 |
| 1199 | 828 | 371 | 33.3 |
| 943 | 697 | · 246 | 28.7 |
| 1105 | 868 | 237 | 23.2 |
| $m$   1090 | 834 | 260 | 25.2 |
| | | | P.E.$_m$=1.9 |

B

| | L | WL | Δ | . Q |
|---|------|------|-----|------|
| | 902 | 564 | 338 | 40.3 |
| | 793 | 517 | 276 | 37.9 |
| | 848 | 639 | 209 | 26.5 |
| | 871 | 709 | 162 | 20.1 |
| | 1034 | 649 | 385 | 39.7 |
| | 745 | 728 | 17 | 2.5 |
| | 975 | 645 | 330 | 36.2 |
| | 805 | 766 | 39 | 5.3 |
| *m* | 872 | 652 | 220 | 26.1 |
| | | | | P.E.$_m$=4 |

C

| | L | WL | Δ | Q |
|---|------|------|-----|------|
| | 1246 | 922 | 324 | 27.9 |
| | 1334 | 1097 | 237 | 19.0 |
| | 1293 | 939 | 354 | 21.0 |
| | 1401 | 988 | 413 | 31.4 |
| | 1214 | 992 | 222 | 19.7 |
| | 1299 | 1045 | 254 | 20.9 |
| | 1358 | 1047 | 311 | 24.4 |
| | 1305 | 881 | 424 | 34.8 |
| *m* | 1306 | 989 | 317 | 24.9 |
| | | | | P.E.$_m$=1.6 |

The average of the total 26 savings of work, stated in per cents, is 25.4 (P.E.$_m$=1.3).

VII. 31 days.   45 tests; 20 at the time A, 15 at B, 10 at C.

A

| L | WL | $\varDelta$ | Q |
|---|---|---|---|
| 1069 | 813 | 256 | 26.0 |
| 1109 | 785 | 324 | 31.6 |
| 1268 | 858 | 410 | 34.7 |
| 1280 | 902 | 378 | 31.6 |
| 1180 | 848 | 332 | 30.3 |
| 1095 | 888 | 207 | 20.5 |
| 1089 | 988 | 101 | 10.1 |
| 1113 | 1043 | 70 | 6.8 |
| 1090 | 1025 | 65 | 6.5 |
| 997 | 876 | 121 | 13.3 |
| 1116 | 934 | 182 | 17.7 |
| 1060 | 893 | 167 | 17.1 |
| 930 | 796 | 134 | 15.9 |
| 1030 | 769 | 261 | 27.6 |
| 980 | 862 | 118 | 13.2 |
| 1079 | 805 | 274 | 27.6 |
| 1254 | 978 | 276 | 23.6 |
| 1164 | 938 | 226 | 20.9 |
| 1127 | 869 | 258 | 24.8 |
| 1268 | 972 | 296 | 25.0 |
| *m*  1115 | 892 | 223 | 21.2 |
| | | | P.E.$_m$=1.3 |

B

| L | WL | $\varDelta$ | Q |
|---|---|---|---|
| 831 | 638 | 193 | 25.2 |
| 867 | 516 | 351 | 43.7 |
| 960 | 748 | 212 | 23.7 |
| 828 | 675 | 153 | 20.0 |
| 859 | 705 | 154 | 19.4 |
| 838 | 661 | 177 | 22.9 |
| 946 | 887 | 59 | 6.7 |
| 833 | 780 | 53 | 6.9 |
| 696 | 532 | 164 | 25.9 |
| 757 | 626 | 131 | 18.9 |
| 906 | 733 | 173 | 20.5 |
| 1024 | 915 | 109 | 11.4 |
| 930 | 780 | 150 | 17.3 |
| 899 | 756 | 143 | 17.1 |
| 1018 | 705 | 313 | 32.8 |
| *m*  879 | 710 | 169 | 20.8 |
| | | | P.E.$_m$=1.4 |

C

| L | WL | $\Delta$ | Q |
|---|---|---|---|
| 1424 | 1004 | 420 | 31.4 |
| 1307 | 1102 | 205 | 16.4 |
| 1351 | 893 | 458 | 36.2 |
| 1245 | 1090 | 155 | 13.4 |
| 1258 | 895 | 363 | 31.0 |
| 1155 | 1070 | 85 | 7.9 |
| 1219 | 800 | 419 | 36.9 |
| 1278 | 1110 | 168 | 14.1 |
| 1120 | 1051 | 69 | 6.7 |
| 1250 | 1055 | 195 | 16.7 |
| *m* 1261 | 1007 | 254 | 21.1 |
|  |  |  | $P.E._m=2.7$ |

The average of 45 savings of work expressed in per cents=21.1 ($P.E._m=0.8$).

A hasty glance at the figures above reveals the fact that for each interval of time the savings in work which become evident when the series is relearned have very fluctuating values. (This saving in work is each time the measure for the amount remembered at the end of the interval.) This is especially the case with their absolute values ($\Delta$), but is also the case with the relative values (Q). The results are taken from the earlier period and suffer from several disturbing influences to which my attention was first drawn by the tests themselves.

In spite of all irregularities in detail, however, they group themselves as a whole with satisfactory certainty into an harmonious picture. As a proof of this the absolute amount of the saving in work is of less value. The latter evidently depends upon the time of day—*i.e.*, upon the changes in the time of the first learning dependent upon it. When this change is greatest (time C), $\Delta$ also is greatest; for the time B, they are in ¾ of the cases larger than for the time A (after multiplying by 4/3). On the other hand, the values (Q) found for the relation of each saving of work to the time originally spent, are apparently almost independent of this ratio. Their averages are close together for all three times of day, and do not show any character of increase or decrease in the later hours. Accordingly I here tabulate the latter.

| No. | I<br>After X<br>hours | II<br>So much of the series<br>learned was retained that<br>in relearning a saving of<br>Q% of the time of original<br>learning was made | III<br>P.E.m | IV<br>The amount forgotten<br>was thus equivalent to<br>v % of the original in<br>terms of time of learning |
|---|---|---|---|---|
|  | X= | Q= |  | v= |
| 1 | 0.33 | 58.2 | 1 | 41.8 |
| 2 | 1. | 44.2 | 1 | 55.8 |
| 3 | 8.8 | 35.8 | 1 | 64.2 |
| 4 | 24. | 33.7 | 1.2 | 66.3 |
| 5 | 48. | 27.8 | 1.4 | 72.2 |
| 6 | 6 x 24 | 25.4 | 1.3 | 74.6 |
| 7 | 31 x 24 | 21.1 | 0.8 | 78.9 |

## Section 29.  Discussion of Results

1. It will probably be claimed that the fact that forgetting would be very rapid at the beginning of the process and very slow at the end should have been foreseen. However, it would be just as reasonable to be surprised at this initial rapidity and later slowness as they come to light here under the definite conditions of our experiment for a certain individual, and for a series of 13 syllables. One hour after the end of the learning, the forgetting had already progressed so far that one half the amount of the original work had to be expended before the series could be reproduced again; after 8 hours the work to be made up amounted to two thirds of the first effort. Gradually, however, the process became slower so that even for rather long periods the additional loss could be ascertained only with difficulty. After 24 hours about one third was always remembered; after 6 days about one fourth, and after a whole month fully one fifth of the first work persisted in effect. The decrease of this after-effect in the latter intervals of time is evidently so slow that it is easy to predict that a complete vanishing of the effect of the first memorisation of these series would, if they had been left to themselves, have occurred only after an indefinitely long period of time.

2. Least satisfactory in the results is the difference between the third and fourth values, especially when taken in connection with the greater difference between the fourth and fifth numbers. In the period 9-24 hours the decrease of the after-effect would

accordingly have been 2½ per cent.  In the period 24 to 48 hours it would have been 6.1 per cent; in the later 24 hours, then, about three times as much as in the earlier 15.  Such a condition is not credible, since in the case of all the other numbers the decrease in the after-effect is greatly retarded by an increase in time.  It does not become credible even under the plausible assumption that night and sleep, which form a greater part of the 15 hours but a smaller part of the 24, retard considerably the decrease in the after-effect.

Therefore it must be assumed that one of these three values is greatly affected by accidental influences.  It would fit in well with the other observations to consider the number 33.7 per cent for the relearning after 24 hours as somewhat too large and to suppose that with a more accurate repetition of the tests it would be 1 to 2 units smaller.  However, it is upheld by observations to be stated presently, so that I am in doubt about it.

3. Considering the special, individual, and uncertain character of our numerical results no one will desire at once to know what "law" is revealed in them.  However, it is noteworthy that all the seven values which cover intervals of one third of an hour in length to 31 days in length (thus from singlefold to 2,000fold) may with tolerable approximation be put into a rather simple mathematical formula.  I call:

$t$ the time in minutes counting from one minute before the end of the learning,

$b$ the saving of work evident in relearning, the equivalent of the amount remembered from the first learning expressed in percentage of the time necessary for this first learning,

$c$ and $k$ two constants to be defined presently

Then the following formula may be written:

$$b = \frac{100\,k}{(\log t)^c + k}$$

By using common logarithms and with merely approximate estimates, not involving exact calculation by the method of least squares,

$k = 1.84$

$c = 1.25$

Then the results are as follows:

| $t$ | $b$ Observed | $b$ Calculated | $\varDelta$ |
|---|---|---|---|
| 20 | 58.2 | 57.0 | + 1.2 |
| 64 | 44.2 | 46.7 | — 2.5 |
| 526 | 35.8 | 34.5 | + 1.3 |
| 1440 | 33.7 | 30.4 | + 3.3 |
| 2 x 1440 | 27.8 | 28.1 | — 0.3 |
| 6 x 1440 | 25.4 | 24.9 | + 0.5 |
| 31 x 1440 | 21.1 | 21.2 | — 0.1 |

The deviations of the calculated values from the observed values surpass the probable limits of error only at the second and fourth values. With regard to the latter I have already expressed the conjecture that the test might have given here too large a value; the second suffers from an uncertainty concerning the correction made. By the determination made for $t$, the formula has the advantage that it is valid for the moment in which the learning ceases and that it gives correctly $b = 100$. In the moment when the series can just be recited, the relearning, of course, requires no time, so that the saving is equal to the work expended.

Solving the formula for $k$ we have

$$k = \frac{b \, (\log t)^c}{100 - b}$$

This expression, $100 - b$ the complement of the work saved, is nothing other than the work required for relearning, the equivalent of the amount forgotten from the first learning. Calling this, $v$, the following simple relation results:

$$\frac{b}{v} = \frac{k}{(\log t)^c}$$

To express it in words: when nonsense series of 13 syllables each were memorised and relearned after different intervals, the quotients of the work saved and the work required were about inversely proportional to a small power of the logarithm of those intervals of time. To express it more briefly and less accurately: the quotients of the amounts retained and the amounts forgotten were inversely as the logarithms of the times.

Of course this statement and the formula upon which it rests have here no other value than that of a shorthand statement of the above results which have been found but once and under the circumstances described. Whether they possess a more general significance so that, under other circumstances or with other individuals, they might find expression in other constants I cannot at the present time say.

## *Section 30. Control Tests*

At any rate, even though only for my own case, I can to a certain extent give support to two of the values mentioned by tests which were made at other periods.

From a period even further back than that of the investigations above mentioned I possess several tests with series of ten syllables, fifteen series composing one test. The series were first memorised and then, at an average of 18 minutes after the first learning, each series was relearned. Six tests had the following results :—

| L | LW | $\Delta$ | Q* |
|---|---|---|---|
| 848 | 436 | 412 | 57.5 |
| 963 | 535 | 428 | 50.9 |
| 921 | 454 | 467 | 58.5 |
| 879 | 444 | 435 | 57.5 |
| 912 | 443 | 469 | 59.4 |
| 821 | 461 | 360 | 51.6 |
| $m = 891$ | 462 | 429 | 56.0<br>P.E.$_m$=1 |

\* The time subtracted from the L when calculating the Q for two reproductions of 15 series is 123 seconds.

When relearning series of ten syllables each, 18 minutes after the first memorisation, 56 per cent of the work originally expended was therefore saved. The number agrees satisfactorily with the one found above (p. 68) for the relearning of series of syllables of 13 syllables each after 19 minutes, 58 per cent. Also the fact that the latter, notwithstanding the longer interval, is still a little greater, harmonises completely, as will be seen, with the results of the next chapter. According to them, shorter series, when memorised, are forgotten a little more quickly than longer ones.

From the period of 1883-84, I have seven tests, consisting of
nine series of 12 syllables each that were relearned 24 hours after
the first memorisation.  The following results were obtained:

|   | L | LW | Δ | Q |
|---|---|---|---|---|
| | 791 | 508 | 283 | 37.9 |
| | 750 | 522 | 228 | 32.3 |
| | 911 | 533 | 378 | 43.6 |
| | 725 | 494 | 231 | 33.9 |
| | 783 | 593 | 190 | 27.1 |
| | 879 | 585 | 294 | 35.2 |
| | 689 | 535 | 154 | 23.9 |
| $m$ | 790 | 539 | 251 | 33.4 |
| | | | | P.E.$_m$=1.7 |

The after-effect of the first memorisation still noticeable after
24 hours, was here equivalent to a saving of work of 33.4 per cent
of the first expenditure.  This number also agrees satisfactorily
with the one communicated above for the relearning of series
of 13 syllables each after 24 hours (33.7 per cent), although
these two were obtained at far separated time-periods and in the
course of widely different investigations.

## CHAPTER VIII

## RETENTION AS A FUNCTION OF REPEATED
## LEARNING

### Section 31. Statement of the Problem and the Investigation

Series of syllables which have been learned by heart, forgotten, and learned anew must be similar as to their inner conditions at the times when they can be recited. The energy of the ideational activity which is directed upon them and which serves to establish them is in both cases so far heightened that quite similar combinations of movements occur in connection with them. For the period after the recital this inner similarity ceases. The series are gradually forgotten, but—as is sufficiently well known—the series which have been learned twice fade away much more slowly than those which have been learned but once. If the relearning is performed a second, a third or a greater number of times, the series are more deeply engraved and fade out less easily and finally, as one would anticipate, they become possessions of the soul as constantly available as other image-series which may be meaningful and useful.

I have attempted to obtain numerical data on the relation of dependence which exists between the permanence of retention of a series and the number of times it has been brought, by means of renewed learning, to a just possible reproduction. The relation is quite similar to that described in Chapter VI as existing between the surety of the series and the number of its repetitions. In the present case, however, the repetitions do not take place all at once, but at separate times and in ever decreasing frequency. On account of our limited insight into the inner connection of these processes we would not be justified in venturing an assertion about one relation on the basis of the other.

Only one value of the time interval between the separate relearnings was chosen, namely, 24 hours. Instead of changing intervals, series of different lengths were chosen for the investi-

gation, the lengths being 12, 24 and 36 syllables. A single test
consisted of nine series of the first length, or three of the second,
or two of the third. In addition to this I carried out several
tests with six stanzas of Byron's "Don Juan."

The plan of the experiment was, then, as follows: The required
number of series was first learned and then, at the same hour
on successive days, it was relearned to the point of first possible
reproduction. In the case of the series of syllables, the number
of days was six; in the case of Byron's stanzas, it was only four.
Thus, on the fifth day, the stanzas were correctly repeated
without any preliminary reproduction and the problem, accordingly, no longer existed. For each kind of series, seven trials
were employed. The total number of separate tests was, in consequence, 154, a number of which required only a few minutes
for their execution.

The entries of the following tables indicate the repetitions
which were necessary in order to bring the series concerned to
the first possible reproduction (including this); the Roman figures designate the successive days.

1. Nine series of 12 syllables each.

| I | II | III | IV | V | VI |
|---|---|---|---|---|---|
| 158 | 102 | 71 | 50 | 38 | 30 |
| 151 | 107 | 74 | 42 | 34 | 30 |
| 175 | 105 | 84 | 60 | 36 | 33 |
| 149 | 102 | 72 | 54 | 35 | 28 |
| 163 | 124 | 69 | 61 | 35 | 31 |
| 173 | 117 | 86 | 64 | 42 | 37 |
| 138 | 106 | 71 | 59 | 37 | 30 |
| *m* 158 | 109 | 75 | 56 | 37 | 31 |
| P.E.$_m$ 3.4 | 2 | 1.7 | 2 | 0.7 | 0.7 |

2. Three series of 24 syllables each.

| I | II | III | IV | V | VI |
|---|---|---|---|---|---|
| 122 | 73 | 45 | 29 | 21 | 16 |
| 127 | 73 | 40 | 25 | 18 | 15 |
| 154 | 78 | 47 | 27 | 18 | 12 |
| 139 | 61 | 33 | 17 | 12 | 10 |
| 133 | 73 | 36 | 26 | 18 | 14 |
| 142 | 66 | 42 | 26 | 17 | 14 |
| 124 | 70 | 36 | 24 | 16 | 14 |
| *m* 134 | 71 | 40 | 25 | 17 | 14 |
| P.E.$_m$ 2.9 | 1.4 | 1.3 | 1 | 0.7 | 0.5 |

3. Two series of 36 syllables each.

| I | II | III | IV | V | VI |
|---|---|---|---|---|---|
| 115 | 52 | 23 | 18 | 9 | 8 |
| 124 | 59 | 33 | 21 | 12 | 10 |
| 137 | 55 | 26 | 17 | 12 | 8 |
| 109 | 48 | 21 | 16 | 10 | 10 |
| 87 | 39 | 21 | 15 | 13 | 8 |
| 105 | 40 | 22 | 17 | 12 | 10 |
| 110 | 41 | 21 | 16 | 10 | 11 |
| $m$  112 | 48 | 24 | 17 | 11 | 9 |
| P.E.$_m$ 4 | 2 | 1.1 | 0.5 | 0.4 | 0.3 |

4. Six stanzas of Byron's "Don Juan" (Canto X).

| I | II | III | IV |
|---|---|---|---|
| 53 | 29 | 18 | 11 |
| 56 | 29 | 16 | 10 |
| 53 | 30 | 15 | 10 |
| 49 | 25 | 14 | 9 |
| 53 | 27 | 16 | 10 |
| 53 | 34 | 21 | 9 |
| 50 | 28 | 17 | 10 |
| $m$  52 | 29 | 17 | 10 |
| P.E.$_m$0.6 | 0.7 | 0.6 | 0.2 |

In order to bring out more clearly the separate relations which exist between the resulting averages, it is necessary to reduce the total figures to the same unit—*i.e.*, to divide them in each case by the number of series constituting a single trial. If this is done and the repetition necessary for the recital is deducted, the following table results, fractions being given to the nearest half or quarter.

| Number of syllables in one series | Number of repetitions which, on the average, were necessary for the bare learning of the series on successive days | | | | | |
|---|---|---|---|---|---|---|
| | I | II | III | IV | V | VI |
| 12 | 16.5 | 11. | 7.5 | 5. | 3. | 2.5 |
| 24 | 44. | 22.5 | 12.5 | 7.5 | 4.5 | 3.5 |
| 36 | 55. | 23. | 11. | 7.5 | 4.5 | 3.5 |
| 1 stanza D. J. | 7.75 | 3.75 | 1.75 | 0.5 | (0). | (0). |

From several points of view these numbers require further consideration.

## Section 32. *Influence of the Length of the Series*

If the results for the first and second days are examined, welcome, though not surprising, supplementary data on the relation of dependence presented in Chapter V is obtained. In the former chapter, it was shown that, as the length of the series increased, the number of repetitions requisite increased very rapidly. Here, the result is that the effect of this need of more numerous repetitions in the cases investigated consists not merely in making the series just reproducible, but also in the firmer establishment of the longer series. After an interval of 24 hours they could be relearned to the point of being just reproducible with a saving both absolutely and relatively greater than with the shorter series.

The following table makes this relation clear.

| Number of syllables in one series | Number of repetitions for learning | Saving in repetitions in relearning after 24 hours | Saving in % of requirement for first learning |
|---|---|---|---|
| 12 | 16.5 | 5.5 | 33.3 |
| 24 | 44 | 21.5 | 48.9 |
| 36 | 55 | 32 | 58.2 |

The saving in the case of the shortest of the series investigated is one third for the second learning as compared with the first; while with the longest series, it is six tenths. It can be said, therefore, that by being learned to the first possible reproduction the series of 36 syllables is approximately twice as firmly established as the series of 12 syllables.

In this there is nothing new. On the basis of the familiar experience that that which is learned with difficulty is better retained, it would have been safe to prophesy such an effect from the greater number of repetitions. That which probably would not have been anticipated and which also demands attention, is the more definite determination of this general relation. So far as the numbers go, they seem to show that, between the increase of the repetitions necessary for the first learning and the inner stability of the series effected by them, there is no proportionality. Neither the absolute nor the relative saving of work advances in the same way as the number of repetitions;

the former advance much faster and the latter noticeably more slowly. It cannot, therefore, be said in any exact sense of the words that the more frequently a series needs to be repeated to-day in order to be learned by heart the more repetitions will be saved in its reproduction after 24 hours. The relation in force seems to be much more complicated and its exact determination would require more extensive investigations.

The relation of repetitions for learning and for repeating English stanzas needs no amplification. These were learned by heart on the first day with less than half of the repetitions necessary for the shortest of the syllable series. They acquired thereby so great stability that for their reproduction on the next day proportionally no more work was needed than for the series of 24 syllables—*i.e.*, about half of the first expenditure.

## Section 33.  Influence of Repeated Learning

We will now take into consideration the results for the successive days taken as a whole. On each day the average number of repetitions necessary for the committing of a given series is less than on the preceding day. With the longer series, in whose case the first output of energy is great, the decrease in the amount of work each time necessary to reach the first possible reproduction is proportionally rapid. With the shorter series, where the first output is small, the decrease is proportionally slow. On this account the numbers of repetitions necessary for the different series approach each other more and more. With the series of 24 and 36 syllables this is apparent even from the second day; from the fourth day on, the numbers fall absolutely together. And by the fifth day they have approached very closely to the number of repetitions still necessary, in accordance with the slower decrease, for the learning of the 12-syllable series.

A simple conformity to law cannot be discovered in this successively decreasing necessity for work. The quotients of the necessary repetitions on two successive days approach unity. If the final repetition were not subtracted, as was done in the concluding table of Section 31, but were reckoned in, this approach would be somewhat faster. (In the case of the English stanzas it generally takes place only under these conditions.)

Nevertheless the course of the numbers cannot be described by a simple formula.

Rather is this the case if one takes into consideration, not the gradually decreasing necessity for work, but the just as gradually decreasing saving of work.

| No. | Number of syllables in one series | Number of repetitions saved on learning a series on the following day; average values | | | | |
|---|---|---|---|---|---|---|
| | | I-II | II-III | III-IV | IV-V | V-VI |
| 1 | 12 | 5.5 | 3.5 | 2.5 | 2 | 0.5 |
| 2 | 24 | 21.5 | 10.0 | 5.0 | 3 | 1.0 |
| 3 | 36 | 32.0 | 12.0 | 3.5 | 3 | 1.0 |
| 4 | 1 stanza D. J. | 4.0 | 2.0 | 1.25 | 0.5 | ... |

Of these numerical sequences two—namely, the second and fourth rows—form with great approximation a decreasing geometrical progression with the exponent 0.5. Very slight changes in the numbers would be sufficient fully to bring out this conformity. By slight changes, the first row might also be transformed into a geometrical progression with the exponent 0.6. On the contrary, a large error in the results of investigation would need to be assumed in order to get out of Row 3 any such geometric progression (whose exponent would then be about one third).

If not for all, yet for most, of the results found, the relation can be formulated as follows: If series of nonsense syllables or verses of a poem are on several successive days each time learned by heart to the point of the first possible reproduction, the successive differences in the repetitions necessary for this form approximately a decreasing geometrical progression. In the case of syllable-series of different lengths, the exponents of these progressions were smaller for the longer series and larger for the shorter ones.

Although the tests just described were individually not more protracted than the others, yet relatively they required many days, and the average values were consequently derived from a rather small number of observations. So here, even more than elsewhere, I am unable to affirm that the simple conformity to law approximately realised in the results so far obtained would stand the test of repetition or wider extension of research. I content myself by calling attention to it without emphasis.

## Section 34. *Influence of the Separate Repetitions*

The problem of the present chapter is, as has already been pointed out, closely related to that of Chapter VI. In both cases the investigation concerns the influence of an increasing number of repetitions on the fixation of the series of syllables, a fixation made increasingly stronger thereby. In the former case the total number of repetitions immediately succeeded each other without regard to whether the spontaneous reproduction of the series was obtained through them or to how it was obtained. In this case the repetitions were distributed over several days and the attainment of the first possible reproduction was employed for their apportionment on the separate days. If, now, the results obtained in both cases have, at least for my own personality, any wider validity, we should expect that in so far as they are comparable, they would harmonise. That is, we should expect in this case as in the former that the effect of the later repetitions (therefore, those of the 2nd, 3rd, and later days), would at first be approximately as great as that of the earlier, and later would decrease more and more.

A more exact comparison is in the nature of the case not now possible. In the first place, the series of Chapter VI and the present ones are of different length. In the second place, the detailed ascertainment of the effect of the repetitions of the succssive days taken solely by themselves would be possible only through assumptions which might be plausible enough on the basis of the data presented, but which would be easily controvertible on account of the insecurity of these data.

We found, for example, that nine 12-syllable series were learned on six successive days by means of 158, 109, 75, 56, 37 and 31 repetitions. The effect of the first 158 repetitions is here immediately given in the 109 repetitions of the succeeding day in the difference, 158 — 109. But if we wish to know the intrinsic effect of these 109 repetitions, namely the saving effected by them, on the third day, we could not simply take the difference, 109 — 75. We should need to know, rather, with how many repetitions $(x)$ the series would have been learned on the third day if no repetitions had occurred on the second, and we should then have in the difference, $x - 75$, the separate effect of the 109 repetitions actually given. Since the forgetting increased somewhat from the second to the third day, $x$ would be somewhat greater than 109. In the same way, for the determination of the effect of the 75 repetitions of the third day, we should need to learn in some way or other with how many repetitions ($y$), the series would have been learned by heart on the fourth day which, on the first day, required 158; and on the second, 109. The difference, $y - 56$, would then give the measure of that effect; and so on. For the ascertainment of $x$, the results of Chapter VII give a certain basis. There the result was that, in the case of 13-syllable series, the amount forgotten at the end of 24 hours was to that forgotten at the end of $2 \times 24$ hours as 66 to 72. But the employment of this relation, itself insecure, would be justifiable only in case of the 12-syllable series, and would accordingly not help in the determination of $y$, etc. One could at the best suppose that the resulting quotients would approximate yet more closely to unity.

Accordingly I renounce these uncertain assumptions, and content myself with presenting the relations of the successive repetitions to the successive savings by showing that the presupposed pure effect of the separate repetitions would be represented by somewhat greater and presumably less divergent numbers.

| Number of syllables of each series | The following savings after 24 hours resulted from each repetition on the separate days (in fractions of their own value) | | | | |
|---|---|---|---|---|---|
| | I | II | III | IV | V |
| 12 | 0.31 | 0.31 | 0.25 | 0.34 | 0.16 |
| 24 | 0.47 | 0.44 | 0.38 | 0.32 | 0.16 |
| 36 | 0.57 | 0.50 | 0.29 | 0.35 | 0.18 |

Although the course of these figures, which are, as has been said, inexact as to their absolute values, is tolerably regular in the case of the 24-syllable series only, its general character agrees very well with what would be expected from the results of Chapter IV. The effect of the repetitions is at first approximately constant, the saving in work which results from these repetitions increases accordingly for a while proportional to their number. Gradually the effect becomes less; and finally, when the series has become so firmly fixed that it can be repeated almost spontaneously after 24 hours, the effect is shown to be decidedly less. The results of the fourth and the present chapter, as far as can be seen, support each other.

Nevertheless, there is a noteworthy distinction to which I call attention. We found above (p. 60) that six 12-syllable series, which had been learned at a given time with an average of 410 repetitions, could be learned by heart at the end of 24 hours with, on the average, 41 repetitions. For a single 12-syllable series, accordingly, 68 immediately successive repetitions had the effect of making possible an errorless recital on the following day after 7 repetitions. In the present research with distribution of the repetitions over several days the same effect appears on the fourth day: 9 12-syllable series were learned by heart with 56 repetitions. Each series, therefore, was learned with about 6 repetitions. But the number of repetitions which were necessary for the production of this effect in the case of the nine series amounted to only $158 + 109 + 75 = 342$. For a single series, therefore, the number was 38. For the relearning of a 12-syllable series at a definite time, accordingly, 38 repetitions, distributed in a certain way over the three preceding days, had just as favorable an effect as 68 repetitions made on the day just previous. Even if one makes very great concessions to the uncertainty of numbers based on so few researches, the difference is large enough to be significant. It makes the assumption probable that *with any considerable number of repetitions* a suitable distribution of them over a space of time is decidedly more advantageous than the massing of them at a single time.

With this result, found here for only very limited conditions, the method naturally employed in practice agrees. The schoolboy doesn't force himself to learn his vocabularies and rules altogether at night, but knows that he must impress them again in the morning. A teacher distributes his class lesson not indifferently over the period at his disposal but reserves in advance a part of it for one or more reviews.

# CHAPTER IX

## RETENTION AS A FUNCTION OF THE ORDER OF SUCCESSION OF THE MEMBERS OF THE SERIES

*" How odd are the connections*
*Of human thoughts which jostle in their flight."*

### Section 35. *Association according to Temporal Sequence and its Explanation*

I shall now discuss a group of investigations made for the purpose of finding out the conditions of association. The results of these investigations are, it seems to me, theoretically of especial interest.

The non-voluntary re-emergence of mental images out of the darkness of memory into the light of consciousness takes place, as has already been mentioned, not at random and accidentally, but in certain regular forms in accordance with the so-called laws of association. General knowledge concerning these laws is as old as psychology itself, but on the other hand a more precise formulation of them has remained—characteristically enough— a matter of dispute up to the very present. Every new presentation starts out with a reinterpretation of the contents of a few lines from Aristotle, and according to the condition of our knowledge it is necessary so to do.

Of these " Laws," now—if, in accordance with usage and it is to be hoped in anticipation of the future, the use of so lofty a term is permitted in connection with formulae of so vague a character—of these laws, I say, there is one which has never been disputed or doubted. It is usually formulated as follows: Ideas which have been developed simultaneously or in immediate succession in the same mind mutually reproduce each other, and do this with greater ease in the direction of the original succession and with a certainty proportional to the frequency with which they were together.

90

This form of non-voluntary reproduction is one of the best verified and most abundantly established facts in the whole realm of mental events. It permeates inseparably every form of reproduction, even the so-called voluntary form. The function of the conscious will, for example, in all the numerous reproductions of the syllable-series which we have come to know, is limited to the general purpose of reproduction and to laying hold of the first member of the series. The remaining members follow automatically, so to speak, and thereby fulfill the law that things which have occurred together in a given series are reproduced in the same order.

However, the mere recognition of these evident facts has naturally not been satisfying and the attempt has been made to penetrate into the inner mechanism of which they are the result. If for a moment we try to follow up this speculation concerning the *Why*, before we have gone more than two steps we are lost in obscurities and bump up against the limits of our knowledge of the *How*.

It is customary to appeal for the explanation of this form of association to the nature of the soul. Mental events, it is said, are not passive happenings but the acts of a subject. What is more natural than that this unitary being should bind together in a definite way the contents of his acts, themselves also unified? Whatever is experienced simultaneously or in immediate succession is conceived in one act of consciousness and by that very means its elements are united and the union is naturally stronger in proportion to the number of times they are entwined by this bond of conscious unity. Whenever, now, by any chance one part only of such a related complex is revived, what else can it do than to attract to itself the remaining parts?

But this conception does not explain as much as it was intended to do. For the remaining parts of the complex are not merely drawn forth but they respond to the pull in an altogether definite direction. If the partial contents are united simply by the fact of their membership in a single conscious act and accordingly all in a similar fashion, how does it come about that a sequence of partial contents returns in precisely the same order and not in any chance combination? In order to make this intelligible, one can proceed in two ways.

In the first place it can be said that the connection of the things present simultaneously in a single conscious act is made from each member to its immediate successor but not to members further distant. This connection is in some way inhibited by the presence of intermediate members, but not by the interposition of pauses, provided that the beginning and end of the pause can be grasped in one act of consciousness. Thereby return is made to the facts, but the advantage which the whole plausible appeal to the unitary act of consciousness offered is silently abandoned. For, however much contention there may be over the number of ideas which a single conscious act may comprehend, it is quite certain that, if not always, at least in most cases, we include more than two members of a series in any one conscious act. If use is made of one feature of the explanation, the characteristic of unity, as a welcome factor, the other side, the manifoldness of the members, must be reckoned with, and the right of representation must not be denied it on assumed but unstatable grounds. Otherwise, we have only said,—and it is possible that we will have to be content with that—that it is so because there are reasons for its being so.

There is, consequently, the temptation to use this second form of statement. The ideas which are conceived in one act of consciousness are, it is true, all bound together, but not in the same way. The strength of the union is, rather, a decreasing function of the time or of the number of intervening members. It is therefore smaller in proportion as the interval which separates the individual members is greater. Let $a, b, c, d$ be a series which has been presented in a single conscious act, then the connection of $a$ with $b$ is stronger than that of $a$ with the later $c;$ and the latter again is stronger than that with $d$. If $a$ is in any way reproduced, it brings with it $b$ and $c$ and $d$, but $b$, which is bound to it more closely, must arise more easily and quickly than $c$, which is closely bound to $b$, etc. The series must therefore reappear in consciousness in its original form although all the members of it are connected with each other.

Such a view as this has been logically worked out by Herbart. He sees the basis of the connection of immediately successive ideas not directly in the unity of the conscious act, but in something similar: opposed ideas which are forced together in a unitary mind can be connected only by partial mutual inhibition followed by fusion of what remains. Yet this, for our purpose, is not essential. He proceeds as follows:

" Let a series, *a, b, c, d* . . . be given in perception, then *a*, from the very first moment of the perception and during its continuance, is subjected to inhibition by other ideas present in consciousness. While *a*, already partially withdrawn from full consciousness, is more and more inhibited, *b* comes up. The latter, at first uninhibited, fuses with the retiring *a*. *c* follows and, itself uninhibited, is united with the fast dimming *b* and the still more obscured *a*. In a similar fashion *d* follows and unites itself in varying degrees with *a, b,* and *c*. Thus there originates for each of these ideas a law according to which, after the whole series has been forced out of consciousness for some time, in its own way on its renewed appearance each idea struggles to call up every other idea of the same series. Suppose that *a* arises first, it is more closely connected with *b*, less with *c*, still less with *d*, etc. But, taken in the reverse order *b, c,* and *d*, all in an uninhibited condition, are fused with what remains of *a*. Consequently *a* seeks to bring them completely back to the form of an uninhibited idea; but its effect is quickest and strongest upon *b*, slower on *c* and still slower on *d*, etc. (whereby closer inspection shows that *b* sinks again while *c* is still rising, and that in the same way *c* sinks while *d* rises, etc.). In short, the series runs off as it was originally given. If we suppose, on the contrary, that *c* was the one initially reproduced, then its effect on *d* and the succeeding members is similar to that revealed by *a*—*i.e.,* the series *c, d,* . . . runs off gradually in conformity with its order. *b* and *a*, however, experience an altogether different influence. With their separate conscious residues, the uninhibited *c* had fused; its effect upon *a* and *b* was therefore without loss of power and without delay, but this effect was limited to bringing back the conscious residues of *a* and *b* bound up with it, only a part of *b* and a still smaller part of *a* being recalled to consciousness. This, then, is what happens if the process of recall begins anywhere at the middle of a known series. That which preceded the point of recall rises at once in graded degrees of clearness. That which followed, on the contrary, runs off in the order of the original series. The series, however, never runs backwards, an anagram is never formed out of a well understood word without voluntary effort."[1]

According to this conception, therefore, the associative threads, which hold together a remembered series, are spun not merely between each member and its immediate successor, but beyond intervening members to every member which stands to it in any close temporal relation. The strength of the threads varies with the distance of the members, but even the weaker of them must be considered as relatively of considerable significance.

The acceptance or rejection of this conception is clearly of great importance for our view of the inner connection of mental events, of the richness and complexity of their groupings and organisation. But it is clearly quite idle to contend about the matter if observation is limited to conscious mental life, to the registration of that which whirls around by chance on the surface of the sea of life.

For, according to the hypothesis, the threads which connect one member to its immediate successor although not the only one spun, are, however, stronger than the others. Consequently, they are, in general, as far as appearances in consciousness are concerned, the important ones, and so the only ones to be observed.

On the other hand, the methods which lie at the basis of the researches already described permit the discovery of connections of even less strength. This is done by artificially strengthening these connections until they reach a definite and uniform level of reproducibility. I have, therefore, carried on according to this method a rather large number of researches to test experimentally

---

[1] Herbart, Lehrb. z. Psychol., Sect. 29. A similar "pleasing" view, as he calls it, was developed by Lotze, Metaphysik (1879) p. 527, with the modification that he attempts to eliminate the notion of varying strength of the ideas, which view he rejects. In accordance with the view mentioned first above, he sees the real reason for a faithful repro- duction of a series of ideas in the fact that association is made only from one link to the following link. Accordingly, he teaches, in his Lectures on Psychology (p. 22), "Any two ideas, regardless of con- tent, are associated when they are produced either simultaneously or in immediate succession—*i.e.*, without an intervening link. And upon this can be based without further artifice the special ease with which we reproduce a series of ideas in their proper order but not out of that order. By "further artifice" he seems to mean Herbart's attempt at an arrangement.

in the field of the syllable-series the question at issue, and to trace an eventual dependence of the strength of the association upon the sequence of the members of the series appearing in succession in consciousness.

### Section 36.   *Methods of Investigation of Actual Behavior*

Researches were again carried out with six series of 16-syllables each.   For greater clearness the series are designated with Roman numbers and the separate syllables with Arabic.   A syllable group of the following form constituted, then, each time the material for research:

$$\text{I(1)   I(2)   I(3)} \ldots\ldots\ldots\ldots\ldots\ldots\ldots\ldots\ldots\ldots\ldots\ldots \text{I(15)   I(16)}$$
$$\text{II(1)  II(2)  II(3)} \ldots\ldots\ldots\ldots\ldots\ldots\ldots\ldots\ldots\ldots\ldots\ldots \text{II(15)  II(16)}$$

$$\text{VI(1)} \ldots\ldots\ldots\ldots\ldots\ldots\ldots\ldots\ldots\ldots\ldots\ldots\ldots\ldots\ldots \text{VI(15)  VI(16)}$$

If I learn such a group, each series by itself, so that it can be repeated without error, and 24 hours later repeat it in the same sequence and to the same point of mastery, then the latter repetition is possible in about two thirds of the time necessary for the first.[1]   The resulting saving in work of one third clearly measures the strength of the association formed during the first learning between one member and its immediate successor.

Let us suppose now that the series are not repeated in precisely the same order in which they were learned.   The syllables learned in the order I(1)  I(2)  I(3)  .  .  .  I(15) I(16) may for example be repeated in the order I(1)  I(3)  I(5)

---

[1] I have omitted to present a few tests with series of 16 syllables each from which this number was obtained, because the results of the sixth chapter sufficiently cover this point.   There (p. 55), we saw that six series of 16 syllables each, each series being repeated 32 times, could be memorised after 24 hours in an average of 863 seconds.   32 repetitions are, on an average, just necessary to bring about the first possible reproduction of series of 16 syllables each.   Considering the close proportion which exists between the number of repetitions on a given day and the saving of work on the next, it cannot much matter whether the series were repeated, each 32 times, or were memorised each to the first possible reproduction.   Since the latter requires about 1,270 seconds, the work of repetition on the following day amounts, as stated above, to about two thirds of this time.   The relative saving when 16-syllable series are relearned after 24 hours, is, therefore, scarcely different from that found for series of 12 and 13 syllables (Chapters VII and VIII), while it gradually increases for still greater length of series.

. . . $I(15)$, $I(2)$ $I(4)$ $I(6)$ . . . $I(16)$, and the remaining series with a similar transformation. There will first be, accordingly, a set composed of all the syllables originally in the odd places and then a set of those originally in the even places, the second set immediately following the first. The new 16-syllable series, thus resulting, is then learned by heart. What will happen? Every member of the transformed series was, in the original series, separated from its present immediate neighbor by an intervening member with the exception of the middle term where there is a break. If these intervening members are actual obstructions to the associative connection, then the transformed series are as good as entirely unknown. In spite of the former learning of the series in the original sequence, no saving in work should be expected in the repetition of the transformed series. If on the other hand in the first learning threads of association are spun not merely from each member to its immediate successor but also over intervening members to more distant syllables, there would exist, already formed, certain predispositions for the new series. The syllables now in succession have already been bound together secretly with threads of a certain strength. In the learning of such a series it will be revealed that noticeably less work is required than for the learning of an altogether new series. The work, however, will be greater than in relearning a given series in unchanged order. In this case, again, the saving in work will constitute a measure of the strength of the associations existing between two members separated by a third. If from the original arrangement of the syllables new series are formed by the omission of 2, 3, or more intervening members, analogous considerations result. The derived series will either be learned without any noticeable saving of work, or a certain saving of work will result, and this will be proportionally less as the number of intervening terms increases.

On the basis of these considerations I undertook the following experiment. I constructed six series of 16 syllables each with the latter arranged by chance. Out of each group a new one was then constructed also composed of six series of 16 syllables each. These new groups were so formed that their adjacent syllables had been separated in the original series by either 1, or 2, or 3, or 7 intervening syllables.

If the separate syllables are designated by the positions which they held in the original arrangement, the following scheme results:

```
I(1)  I(2)  I(3)...............................................I(15)  I(16)
II(1) II(2) II(3)..............................................II(15) II(16)
 .                                                              .
 .                                                              .
VI(1)..........................................................VI(16)
```

By using the same scheme the derived groups appear as follows:

By Skipping 1 Syllable
```
I(1)  I(3)  I(5)..............I(15)  I(2)  I(4)  I(6)..............I(16)
II(1) II(3) II(5).............II(15) II(2) II(4) II(6).............II(16)
 .                                                                 .
 .                                                                 .
VI(1) VI(3)...................VI(15) VI(2) VI(4)...................VI(16)
```

By Skipping 2 Syllables
```
I(1)  I(4)  I(7) I(10) I(13) I(16)  I(2)  I(5)  I(8) I(11) I(14)  I(3)  I(6)  I(9) I(12) I(15)
II(1) II(4) II(7)...........II(16) II(2) II(5)...........II(14) II(3) II(6)...........II(15)
 .                                                                  .
VI(1) VI(4).................VI(16) VI(2) VI(5)...........VI(14) VI(3) VI(6)..........VI(15)
```

By Skipping 3 Syllables
```
I(1)  I(5)  I(9) I(13)  I(2)  I(6) I(10) I(14)  I(3)  I(7) I(11) I(15)  I(4)  I(8) I(12) I(16)
II(1) II(5)...........II(2) II(6)...........II(3) II(7)...........II(4) II(8)......II(16)
 .                                                                  .
VI(1) VI(5)...........VI(2) VI(6)...........VI(3) VI(7)...........VI(4) VI(8)......VI(16)
```

By Skipping 7 Syllables
```
I(1)  I(9) II(1) II(9) III(1) III(9) IV(1) IV(9) V(1) V(9) VI(1) VI(9) I(2) I(10) II(2) II(10)
III(2)III(10) IV(2)IV(10) V(2) V(10) VI(2)VI(10)  I(3) I(11) II(3) II(11) III(3)III(11) IV(3)IV(11)
 .
V(7) V(15) VI(7)VI(15)  I(8) I(16) II(8) II(16) III(8)III(16) IV(8)IV(16) V(8) V(16) VI(8)VI(16)
```

As a glance at this scheme will show, not all the neighboring syllables of the derived series were originally separated by the number of syllables designated. In some places in order to again obtain series of 16 syllables, greater jumps were made; but in no case was the interval less. Such places are, for example, in the series in which two syllables are skipped, the transitions from I(16) to I(2) and from I(14) to I(3). In the series in which 7 intermediates were jumped, there are seven places where there was no previous connection between successive syllables since the syllables in question came from different series and the different series, as has been often mentioned, were learned independently. The following is given in illustration: I(9) II(1), II(9) III(1), etc. The number of these breaks varies with the different kinds of derivation, but in each case is the same as the number of skipped syllables. On account of this difference,

the derived series suffer from an inequality inherent in the nature
of the experiment.

In the course of the experiment the skipping of more than 7
syllables was shown to be desirable, but I refrained from carrying that out. The investigations with the six 16-syllable series
were carried quite far; and if series had been constructed using
greater intervals, the breaks above mentioned would have had
too much dominance. The derived series then contained ever
fewer syllable-sequences for which an association was possible
on the basis of the learning of the original arrangement; they
were ever thus more incomparable.

The investigations were carried on as follows:—Each time the
six series were learned in the original order and then 24 hours
later in the derived and the times required were compared. On
account of the limitation of the series to those described above
the results are, under certain circumstances, open to a serious
objection. Let it be supposed that the result is that the derived
series are actually learned with a certain saving of time, then
this saving is not necessarily due to the supposed cause, an association between syllables not immediately adjacent. The argu-
ment might, rather, run as follows. The syllables which are
first learned in one order and after 24 hours in another are in
both cases the same syllables. By means of the first learning
they are impressed not merely in their definite order but also
purely as individual syllables; with repetition they become to
some extent familiar, at least more familiar than other syllables,
which had not been learned just before. Moreover the new
series have in part the same initial and final members as the
old. Therefore, if they are learned in somewhat less time than
the first series required, it is not to be wondered at. The basis
of this does not necessarily lie in the artificial and systematic
change of the arrangement, but it possibly rests merely on the
identity of the syllables. If these were repeated on the second
day in a new arrangement made entirely by chance they would
probably show equally a saving in work.

In consideration of this objection and for the control of the
remaining results I have introduced a further, the fifth, kind of
derived series. The initial and final syllables of the original
series were left in their places. The remaining 84 syllables, intermediates, were shaken up together and then, after chance

drawing, were employed in the construction of new series between the original initial and final series. As a result of the learning of th~ original and derived series there must in this case also be ~vealed how much of the saving in work is to be ascribed merely to the identity of the syllable masses and to the identity of the initial and final members of the separate series.

## Section 37. Results. Associations of Indirect Sequence

For each group of original and derived series 11 double tests were instituted, 55 therefore in all. These were distributed irregularly over about 9 months. The results were as follows:

1) With derivation of the series by skipping one intermediate syllable.

| The original series were learned in x seconds | The corresponding de-rived series, in y seconds | The latter, therefore, with a saving of z seconds |
|---|---|---|
| x= | y= | z= |
| 1187 | 1095 | 92 |
| 1220 | 1142 | 78 |
| 1139 | 1107 | 32 |
| 1428 | 1123 | 305 |
| 1279 | 1155 | 124 |
| 1245 | 1086 | 159 |
| 1390 | 1013 | 377 |
| 1254 | 1191 | 63 |
| 1335 | 1128 | 207 |
| 1266 | 1152 | 114 |
| 1259 | 1141 | 118 |
| *m* 1273 | 1121 | 152 |

2) With derivation of the series by skipping two intermediate syllables.

| x= | y= | z= |
|---|---|---|
| 1400 | 1185 | 215 |
| 1213 | 1252 | —39 |
| 1323 | 1245 | 78 |
| 1366 | 1103 | 263 |
| 1216 | 1066 | 150 |
| 1062 | 1003 | 59 |
| 1163 | 1161 | 2 |
| 1251 | 1204 | 47 |
| 1182 | 1086 | 96 |
| 1300 | 1076 | 224 |
| 1276 | 1339 | —63 |
| *m* 1250 | 1156 | 94 |

3) With derivation of the series by skipping three intermediate syllables.

| The original series were learned in x seconds | The corresponding derived series, in y seconds | The latter, therefore, with a saving of z seconds |
|---|---|---|
| x= | y= | z= |
| 1282 | 1347 | —65 |
| 1202 | 1131 | 71 |
| 1205 | 1157 | 48 |
| 1303 | 1271 | 32 |
| 1132 | 1098 | 34 |
| 1365 | 1235 | 130 |
| 1210 | 1145 | 65 |
| 1364 | 1176 | 188 |
| 1308 | 1175 | 133 |
| 1298 | 1209 | 89 |
| 1286 | 1148 | 138 |
| m  1269 | 1190 | 78 |

4) With derivation of the series by skipping seven intermediate syllables.

| x= | y= | z= |
|---|---|---|
| 1165 | 1086 | 79 |
| 1265 | 1295 | —30 |
| 1197 | 1091 | 106 |
| 1295 | 1254 | 41 |
| 1233 | 1207 | 26 |
| 1335 | 1288 | 47 |
| 1321 | 1278 | 43 |
| 1344 | 1275 | 69 |
| 1322 | 1328 | —6 |
| 1224 | 1212 | 12 |
| 1294 | 1217 | 77 |
| m  1272 | 1230 | 42 |

5) With derivation of the series by retaining the beginning and end syllables and arranging the remainder by chance.

| | | |
|---|---|---|
| 1305 | 1302 | 3 |
| 1181 | 1259 | —78 |
| 1207 | 1237 | —30 |
| 1401 | 1277 | 124 |
| 1278 | 1271 | 7 |
| 1302 | 1301 | 1 |
| 1248 | 1379 | —131 |
| 1237 | 1240 | —3 |
| 1355 | 1236 | 119 |
| 1214 | 1142 | 72 |
| 1147 | 1101 | 46 |
| m  1261 | 1250 | 12 |

To summarize the results: The new series formed by skipping 1, 2, 3 and 7 intermediate members were learned with an average saving of 152, 94, 78 and 42 seconds. In the case of the construction of a new series through a mere permutation of the syllables, there was an average saving of 12 seconds.

In order to determine the significance of these figures, it is necessary to compare them with the saving in work in my case in the relearning of an unchanged series after 24 hours. This amounted to about one third of the time necessary for the first learning in the case of 16-syllable series, therefore about 420 seconds.

This number measures the strength of the connection existing between each member and its immediate sequent, therefore the maximal effect of association under the conditions established. If this is taken as unity, then the strength of the connection of each member with the second following is a generous third and with the third following is a scant fourth.

The nature of the results obtained confirm—for myself and the cases investigated—the second conception given above and explained by means of a quotation from Herbart. With repetition of the syllable series not only are the individual terms associated with their immediate sequents but connections are also established betwen each term and several of those which follow it beyond intervening members. To state it briefly, there seems to be an association not merely in direct but also in indirect succession. The strength of these connections decreases with the number of the intervening numbers; with a small number it was, as will be admitted, of surprising and unanticipated magnitude.

No evidence has been secured, however, establishing the facilitation of the process of relearning a series by means of the identity of the syllables and the identity of the initial and final terms.

## Section 38.  *Experiments with Exclusion of Knowledge*

I have hitherto not stated the probable errors of the results, in order to discuss their reliability more fully at this time.

When I started upon the experiment I had no decided opinion in favor of the final results. I did not find facilitation of the learning of the derived series essentially more plausible than the opposite. As the numbers more and more bespoke the existence

of such facilitation, it dawned upon me that this was the correct
and natural thing. After what has been said above (p. 27ff)
one might think that in the case of the remaining experiments,
this idea has possibly favored a more attentive and therefore
quicker learning of the derived series, and so has, at least,
decidedly strengthened the resulting saving in work, even if it
has not caused it altogether.

For the three largest of the numbers found,—consequently, for
the facilitation of the work which took place in the case of the
omission of 1, 2, and 3 intervening syllables—this objection is of
slight significance. For these are proportionately so large that
it would be attributing too much to an involuntary heightening
of a state of attention, voluntarily concentrated without this to
the utmost, if an actual influence is ascribed to it here. Moreover, the gradation of the numbers, decisively issuing as they do
from the distribution of the individual values and running parallel
with the number of skipped intermediate terms, is inconceivable
on any such hypothesis as this. For the supposed greater concentration of the attention could clearly work only in general.
How could it possibly bring about so regular a gradation of
numbers in the case of tests which were separated from each
other by weeks and months?

The objection presented above could render doubtful only the
fourth result, the proportionally slight saving in the learning of
series formed from other series by skipping seven intermediate
terms.

Clearly in this case the exact determination of the difference
is of especial interest because of the significant size of the interval
over which an association took place.

In the case of the present investigations there exists the possibility of so arranging them that knowledge concerning the outcome of the gradually accumulating results is excluded and so
that consequently the disturbing influence of secret views and
desires disappears. I have accordingly instituted a further group
of 30 double tests in the following way as a control of the above
results, and especially of the least certain of them.

On the front side of a page were written six 16-syllable series
selected by chance and on the reverse side of the same sheet six
series formed from them by one of the methods of derivation
described above (p. 97). For each of the five transforma-

tions 6 sheets were prepared. The fronts and backs of these could be easily distinguished but not the sheets themselves. The thirty sheets were shuffled together and then laid aside until any memory as to the occurrence of the separate syllables in definite transformations could be considered as effaced. Then the front side, and 24 hours later, the reverse side of a given sheet were learned by heart. The times necessary for learning the separate series were noted, but they were not assembled and further elaborated until all 30 sheets had been completed. Following are the numbers.

1) With derivation of series transformed by skipping one intermediate syllable.

| The original series were learned in x seconds | The corresponding derived series, in y seconds | The latter, therefore, with a saving of z seconds |
|---|---|---|
| x= | y= | z= |
| 1137 | 1081 | 56 |
| 1292 | 1045 | 247 |
| 1202 | 1237 | —35 |
| 1272 | 1202 | 70 |
| 1436 | 1299 | 137 |
| 1340 | 1157 | 183 |
| m  1280 | 1170 | 110 |

2) With derivation of the series by skipping two intermediate syllables.

| | | |
|---|---|---|
| x= | y= | z= |
| 1415 | 1232 | 183 |
| 1201 | 1290 | —89 |
| 1291 | 1156 | 135 |
| 1358 | 1153 | 205 |
| 1232 | 1254 | —22 |
| 1168 | 1107 | 61 |
| m  1278 | 1199 | 79 |

3) With derivation of the series by skipping three intermediate syllables

| | | |
|---|---|---|
| x= | y= | z= |
| 1205 | 1166 | 39 |
| 1339 | 1068 | 271 |
| 1179 | 1293 | —114 |
| 1238 | 1196 | 42 |
| 1257 | 1231 | 26 |
| 1240 | 1122 | 118 |
| m  1243 | 1179 | 64 |

4) With derivation of the series by skipping seven intermediate syllables.

| The original series were learned in x seconds | The corresponding derived series, in y seconds | The latter, therefore, with a saving of z seconds |
|---|---|---|
| x= | y= | z= |
| 1191 | 1120 | 71 |
| 1191 | 1185 | 6 |
| 1237 | 1295 | —58 |
| 1350 | 1306 | 44 |
| 1308 | 1260 | 48 |
| 1289 | 1158 | 131 |
| m 1261 | 1221 | 40 |

5) With derivation of the series by retaining the first and last syllables in position and changing the rest by chance.

| x= | y= | z= |
|---|---|---|
| 1305 | 1180 | 125 |
| 1206 | 1205 | 1 |
| 1310 | 1426 | —116 |
| 1163 | 1089 | 74 |
| 1272 | 1388 | —116 |
| 1309 | 1305 | 4 |
| m 1261 | 1266 | —5 |

By derivation of the transformed series by skipping 1, 2, 3, 7 intermediate syllables, the derived series were therefore learned with an average saving of 110, 79, 64, 40 seconds. On the contrary with derivation of the series by permutation of the syllables the learning required an average *increase* in expenditure of 5 seconds.

Taken as a whole, these last results exactly confirm, as can be seen, the result that was obtained at the beginning. The number of these experiments was proportionally small and, during the course of each experiment, there was complete exclusion of knowledge as to results. In spite of these facts and although the numbers, considered individually, seem to be distributed without regard to law, their grouping, when taken as a whole, is seen to be in conformity to a simple law. The fewer are the intervening members which separate two syllables of a series which has been learned by heart, the less is the resistance offered by these separated syllables to their being learned in a new order.

And, in the same way, the fewer are these intervening terms, the stronger are the bonds which, as a result of the learning of the original series, connect the two syllables across the intervening members.

In addition to agreeing in their general course, the numbers for both groups of experiments also agree in the following respect. The difference between the first and second numbers has the greatest value, and that between the second and third has the least value. On the other hand, it is surprising that, with respect to their absolute size, the numbers of the second group are throughout smaller than those of the first. Two causes may be brought forward in explanation of this behavior, which, considering the conformity of the numbers, can scarcely be accidental. It may be that here is actually revealed that influence of expectation which has already been mentioned. On the basis of this hypothesis, the explanation of the fact that the numbers of the first group come out somewhat too large is that, in the course of the experiment, the existence of a saving in work in the case of the derived series was anticipated, and for this reason the learning of the series took place involuntarily with a somewhat greater concentration of attention. On the other hand, it may be that, in consequence of the excluded knowledge, there has been at work in the case of the numbers of the second group a disturbing element which has made them smaller. Here, to be sure, during the learning of the derived series a very lively curiosity developed concerning the category of transformation to which the series which had just been learned belonged. That this must have had a distracting, and therefore retarding, influence is probable not only in itself but also through the result obtained from the series derived by permutation of syllables. It was to be expected that the identity of the syllables, as well as of the initial and end terms, would make itself felt in this case by a saving of work, however small that saving might be. The latter effect appears, it is true, in the experiments of the first group. With those of the second group, however, there is noticeable, instead of this saving of work, a slight additional expenditure of time. This, if it is not merely accidental, can scarcely be explained otherwise than through the distracting curiosity mentioned.

It is possible that both influences were at work simultaneously so that the first experiments gave results which were somewhat too high; and the second, results that were somewhat too low. It is allowable, under this hypothesis, to put the two sets of figures together so that the contrasting errors may compensate each other. In this way there was finally obtained out of the 85 double tests the following table.

| Number of intermediate syllables skipped in the formation of the derived series | Time for learning the original series | Time for learning the derived series | Saving of work in learning the derived series | Probable error of saving of work* | Saving of work in % of original learning time |
|---|---|---|---|---|---|
| | (The numbers of the four middle columns denote seconds) | | | | |
| 0 | (1266) | (844) | (422) | | (33.3) |
| 1 | 1275 | 1138 | 137 | ± 16 | 10.8 |
| 2 | 1260 | 1171 | 89 | ± 18 | 7.0 |
| 3 | 1260 | 1186 | 73 | ± 13 | 5.8 |
| 7 | 1268 | 1227 | 42 | ± 7 | 3.3 |
| permutation of syllables | 1261 | 1255 | 6 | ± 13 | 0.5 |

* The probable errors are calculated from the separate values for savings of work, while the latter, which were actually obtained by subtraction, are considered as the results of direct observation. (See p. 67, note.)

## Section 39. Discussion of Results

In the foregoing table an especial interest, it seems to me, is connected with the last, and also with the next to the last, row of numbers. When there was complete identity of all the syllables and the initial and end terms were left in their places, the average saving of time for 17 tests dealing with the learning of the derived series was so slight that it was hardly to be determined. It fell within half of its probable error. The syllables were, therefore, in themselves, outside of their connection, so familiar to me that they did not become noticeably more familiar after being repeated 32 times. On the contrary when a related series was repeated the same number of times, each syllable became so firmly bound to the syllable which followed 8 places beyond that 24 hours later the influence of this connection could be determined in no doubtful fashion. It attains a value 6 times the probable error. Its existence, therefore, must be considered to be fully proved although naturally we cannot be so sure that its size is exactly what it was found to be in the experiments. Although its absolute value is small, yet its influence amounts to one tenth of that of the connection which binds every member to its immediate successor. It is so significant, and at the same time the decrease in the after-effect of connections which were formed over 2, 3, 7 intervening members is so gradual a one, that the assertion can be made, on these grounds alone, that even the terms which stand still further from one another may have been bound to each other subconsciously by threads of noticeable strength at the time of the learning of the series.

I will summarise the results so far given in a theoretical generalisation. As a result of the repetition of the syllable-series certain connections are established between each member and all those that follow it. These connections are revealed by the fact that the syllable-pairs so bound together are recalled to mind more easily and with the overcoming of less friction than similar pairs which have not been previously united. The strength of the connection, and therefore the amount of work which is eventually saved, is a decreasing function of the time or of the number of the intervening members which separated the syllables in question from one another in the original series. It is a maximum for immediately successive members. The precise character of the function is unknown except that it decreases at first quickly and then gradually very slowly with the increasing distance of the terms.

If the abstract but familiar conceptions of 'power,' 'disposition,' be substituted for the concrete ideas of saving in work and easier reproduction, the matter can be stated as follows. As a result of the learning of a series each member has a tendency, a latent disposition, to draw after itself, at its own return to consciousness, all the members of the series which followed it. These tendencies are of varying strength. They are the strongest for the members which immediately follow. These tendencies are accordingly in general most easily demonstrable in consciousness. The series will return in its original form without the intervention of other influences while the forces directed to the resuscitation of the remaining members can be explicitly demonstrated only by the introduction of other conditions.

It is naturally not conceivable that by a mere caprice of
nature the validity of the principles discovered should be limited
exclusively to the character of the material in which they were
obtained—*i.e.,* to series of nonsense syllables. They may be
assumed to hold in an analogous way for every kind of idea-
series and for the parts of any such series. It goes without
saying, wherever relations exist between the separate ideas,
other than those of temporal sequence and separation by intermediate members, these forces will control the associative flow,
not exclusively, but with reference to all the modifications and
complications introduced by relations of various affinities, connection, meaning, and the like.

At any rate, it will not be denied that the doctrine of Association would gain through a general validity of these results a
genuine rounding out and, so to say, a greater reasonableness.
The customary formulation, "ideas become associated if they
are experienced simultaneously or in immediate succession," has
something irrational about it. If the immediacy of succession
is taken precisely, the principle contradicts the most common
experiences. If it is not taken exactly, then it is hard to state
what kind of sequence is properly meant. At the same time
it is not clear why a sequence not quite direct should have an
advantage which suddenly disappears in the case of a sequence
still more indirect. As we now know, the directness or indirect-
ness of the sequence is without effect upon the general nature of
what happens between ideas which succeed each other. In both
cases connections are formed which on account of their complete similarity can be designated only by the common term,
Association. But these are of different strength. As the succession of united ideas approaches ideal immediacy the connect-
ing threads grow stronger, and in proportion as it departs from
this ideal, these threads grow weaker. The associations between
more distant terms, although actually present and demonstrable
under proper conditions have, nevertheless, on account of their
slight strength, practically no significance. The associations
between adjacent terms are, on the contrary, of relatively great
importance, and will make their influence abundantly felt. Of.
course, if the series were left entirely to themselves and if they
were always produced in precisely the same order, for each
term there would appear only one association, the relatively

strongest—namely, that with the immediately succeeding term. But series of ideas are never left to themselves. The rich and quickly changing order of events brings them into the most manifold relations. They return with their members in the most varied combinations. And then, under certain circumstances, the stronger of these less strong associations between more distant terms must find opportunity to authenticate their existence and to enter into the inner course of events in an effective way. It is easy to see how they must favor a more rapid growth, a richer differentiation, and a many-sided ramification of the ideas which characterise the controlled mental life. Of course they also favor a greater manifoldness, and so apparently a greater arbitrariness and irregularity, in mental events.

Before I proceed further, I wish to add a few words concerning the above mentioned (p. 91) derivation of the association of successive ideas from the unitary consciousness of a unitary soul. There is a certain danger in bringing together a present result with one found previously. I mentioned above (p. 47) that the number of syllables which I can repeat without error after a single reading is about *seven*. One can, with a certain justification, look upon this number as a measure of the ideas of this sort which I can grasp in a single unitary conscious act. As we just now saw, associations are formed of noticeable strength over more than seven intervening members, therefore between the beginning and end of a nine-syllable series. And on account of the size of the numbers obtained and the nature of their gradation, it seems probable that, even with a larger number of syllables, connections would be formed between their extremes. If, however, associations are built between members too far separated to be held together in a single conscious act, it is no longer possible to explain the presence of those associations on the basis of the simultaneous presence of the united ideas in consciousness.

However, I recognise that those for whom such a derivation is a cherished matter are not necessarily forced by the above discussion to abandon their conception. Such are those who consider the unitary acts of a unitary soul as something more original, intelligible, transparent or better worthy of belief than the simple facts of association described above, so that the reduction of the latter to the former would be a noteworthy

achievement. One needs but to say that, in the case of an
unfamiliar sequence of syllables, only about seven can be
grasped in one act, but that with frequent repetition and gradually increasing familiarity with the series this capacity of consciousness may be increased. So, for example, a series of 16
syllables, which have been thoroughly memorised, may be present
in a single conscious act. Accordingly this "explanation" is
freely available. Those for whom it was of value in the case
of association by simultaneity or immediate succession can
employ it fully as well for our case of indirect sequence. And
because of the modest requirements which in psychology are so
often imposed upon explanations, this view will doubtless for
a long time serve to make dim the vision and so prevent the
frank recognition of this as one of the most wonderful of all
riddles, and it will also act as a hindrance in the search for its
true understanding.

## Section 40.  Reverse Associations

Of the many problems which spring out of the results presented, I have been able for the time being to investigate only
a few and these by means of only a small number of experiments.

As a result of the frequent repetition of a series—*a, b, c, d*
. . .  —certain connections—*ab, ac, ad, bd,* etc.—are
formed. The idea *a,* whenever and however it returns to consciousness, has certain tendencies of different strength to bring
also with it to consciousness the ideas *b, c, d.* Are now these
connections and tendencies reciprocal? That is, if at any time
*c* and not *a* is the idea by some chance revived, does this have,
in addition to the tendency to bring *d* and *e* back with it, a
similar tendency in the reverse direction towards *b* and *a?* In
other words:—As a result of the previous learning of *a, b, c, d,*
the sequences *a, b, c; a, c, e,* are more easily learned than any
grouping of equal length of syllables previously unknown such
as *p, q, r.* . . . Is the same thing true of the sequences
*c b a,* and *e c a?* As a result of manifold repetition of a series
are associations also formed in the reverse order?

The views of the psychologists seem to be divergent upon this
point. One side call attention to the undoubted fact that in
spite of complete mastery of, say, the Greek alphabet a person

is not at all in a position to repeat it readily backwards if he has not specially studied and practiced it in this form.

The other side make extensive use of reverse associations, as of something quite intelligible, in their explanation of the origin of voluntary and purposive movements. According to them the movements of the child are at first involuntary and accidental. With certain combinations of these, intensely pleasurable feelings result. In the case of movements as of feelings, memory traces remain which, by repetition of the occurrences, are always more closely associated with each other. If this connection has attained a certain strength, the mere idea of the agreeable feeling leads backwards to the idea of the movement which aroused it; then comes the actual movement and with it also the actual sensed feeling.

The conception of Herbart, which we learned to know above (p. 94), holds the middle course between these two views. The idea $c$, which appears in the course of a series, fuses with the ideas $b$ and $a$, which have preceded it and which are yet present although becoming dim. If $c$ is later on reproduced, it brings $b$ and $a$ with it but dimmed, not fully uninhibited or clearly conscious. With the sudden arousal of a member out of the midst of a series we survey that which preceded " at once in graded clearness "; but never does it happen that the series runs off in reverse order. To the member which springs up in consciousness there succeed in due order and in complete consciousness those terms which followed it in the original series.

For the purpose of testing the actual relations I carried out an experiment entirely similar to the previously described investigations. Out of groups each composed of six 16-syllable series arranged by chance, new groups were derived either through mere reversal of the sequence or by that plus the skipping of an intermediate syllable. Then the two sets of groups were learned by heart, the derived form 24 hours later than the original.

If the scheme for the original form is written as follows:

I(1) I(2) I(3)......I(15) I(16), then the corresponding derived series is thus designated:

In the case of mere reversal of the syllable sequence;

I(16) I(15) I(14).......I(2) I(1),

In the case of reversal plus skipping of an intermediate syllable,
I(16) I(14) I(12)....I(4) I(2) I(15) I(13)....I(3) I(1).
For the first kind of derivation I have carried out ten experiments; for the second, only four.

The results are as follows:

1) With derivation of the transformed series by mere reversal of the syllable sequence.

| The original series were learned in x seconds | The corresponding derived series, in y seconds | The latter, therefore, with a saving of z seconds |
|---|---|---|
| x= | y= | z= |
| 1172 | 1023 | 149 |
| 1317 | 1170 | 147 |
| 1213 | 977 | 236 |
| 1202 | 1194 | 8 |
| 1257 | 1031 | 226 |
| 1210 | 1087 | 123 |
| 1285 | 1051 | 234 |
| 1260 | 1150 | 110 |
| 1245 | 1070 | 175 |
| 1329 | 1189 | 140 |
| m  1249 | 1094 | 155 P.E._m=15 |

In relation to the time of learning the original series the saving amounts to 12.4 per cent.

2) With derivation of the transformed series by reversal and at the same time by skipping one intermediate syllable.

| x= | y= | z= |
|---|---|---|
| 1337 | 1291 | 46 |
| 1255 | 1164 | 91 |
| 1158 | 1143 | 15 |
| 1313 | 1224 | 89 |
| m  1266 | 1206 | 60 P.E._m=12 |

In relation to the time of learning the original series the saving amounted to 5 per cent.

As a result of the learning of a series certain connections of the members are therefore actually formed in a reverse as well as in a forward direction. These connections are revealed in this way, that series which are formed out of members thus

connected are more easily learned than similar series, whose
individual members are just as familiar but which have not
been previously connected. The strength of the predispositions
thus created was again a decreasing function of the distance of
the members from each other in the original series. It was,
however, considerably less for the reverse connections than for
the forward ones, the distances being equal. With an approximately equal number of repetitions of the series the member
immediately preceding a given member was not much more
closely associated with it than the second one following it; the
second preceding—so far as may be determined on the basis
of these few researches—scarcely as firmly as the third following.

If one could assume a more general validity for this relation
found here first in connection with syllable series, the mutually
opposed experiences just mentioned would, I believe, become
thoroughly intelligible. Where a series consists of only two
members—as in the case of the connection between a simple
idea of movement and that of an agreeable feeling—then, by
means of frequent repetition the end term will acquire so strong
a tendency to call up after itself the initial term that the latter
will actually appear. For the bringing up of the term first preceding it is the only thing for which, as a result of the many
repetitions, the second term has acquired a predisposition. But,
no matter how many repetitions there may be in the case of a
long series, it will never happen on the arousal of a middle term
that the series will reappear in a reverse order. For, however
easily the immediately preceding term may connect itself with
the one for the moment aroused, the immediately succeeding
term will appear more easily by far, and so will win the victory,
provided other influences do not intervene.

No matter how thoroughly a person may have learned the
Greek alphabet, he will never be in a condition to repeat it
backwards without further training. But if he chances to set
out purposely to learn it backwards, he will probably accomplish
this in noticeably shorter time than was the case in the previous
learning in the customary order. The objection is not in point
that a poem or speech which has been committed to heart is
not necessarily learned more quickly backwards than it was
originally forwards. For with the learning in reverse direction
the numerous threads of inner connection on which rapid learn-

ing of meaningful material in general depends will be brought
to nothing.

## Section 41. The Dependence of Associations of Indirect Sequence upon the Number of Repetitions

The connection set up as a result of many repetitions between
the immediately succeeding members of an idea- or syllable-
series is a function of the number of repetitions. As a result
of the investigations of Chapter VI, which were purposely directed to the discovery of this relation, an approximate proportionality, within tolerably wide limits, has been made out
between the number of repetitions and the strength of the connections established by them. The latter was measured, precisely as in the investigations of the present chapter, by the
amount of work saved in relearning the connected series after
24 hours.

If now, as a result of repetitions, connections are also set
up between members of a series which are not immediately successive, the strength of the latter is naturally also in some way
dependent upon the number of repetitions. The question arises
in what form the different dependence occurs in this case. Does
a proportionality exist here also? If the number of repetitions
is made greater, will the threads of separate strength, which
bind together all the members of a series learned by heart, increase in strength in the same proportion? Or is the nature and
rate of their increase in strength a different one as is the case
with the strength of the threads themselves? On the basis of
our present knowledge neither the one nor the other of these
possibilities can be declared self-evident.

To facilitate an insight into the actual conditions I have instituted a few preliminary experiments in the following way. Six
series of 16 syllables each were impressed upon the memory
by a 16- or 64-fold attentive repetition. After 24 hours an
equal number of derived series of the same length, which had
been obtained from those already learned by skipping one intermediate syllable, were learned by heart to the first repetition.
In order to make the investigations useful in other ways, the
series were derived in this case by a method somewhat different
from that described above (p. 97). The latter method differs

from the former in that here the odd-numbered syllables of the
original series were not followed by the even-numbered syllables
of the same series. But all the odd-numbered syllables of two
original series were united to form a new 16-syllable series.
Then the even-numbered syllables of the same original series
were united to form a second new series. The scheme of the
derived series was therefore not, as above,

I(1)  I(3)  I(5)................................ I(15)  I(2)  I(4)...... I(16),
II(1)  II(3)  II(5)................................ II(15)  II(2)  II(4)...... II(16),

but rather

I(1)  I(3)  I(5)................................ I(15)  II(1)  II(3)...... II(15)
I(2)  I(4)  I(6)................................ I(16)  II(2)  II(4)...... II(16)

The effect of the derivation upon the learning of the derived
series, cannot, as it seems, be essentially affected through this
slight change. Here, as in the above described method of derivation, the syllables which during the first learning had been separated from each other by an intervening syllable were learned
24 hours later in immediate succession.

For each number of repetitions used in learning I made 8
double tests, which gave the following results:

Number of repetitions employed for the impression of each of
the original series:

|  | 16 | 64 |
|---|---|---|

Number of seconds required for learning the six derived series
after 24 hours (including the recital):

| | 16 | 64 |
|---|---|---|
| | 1178 | 1157 |
| | 1216 | 982 |
| | 1216 | 1198 |
| | 950 | 1148 |
| | 1358 | 995 |
| | 1019 | 1017 |
| | 1191 | 1183 |
| | 1230 | 1196 |
| Average | 1170 | 1109 |
| Probable error | 30 | 22 |

On account of the small number of experiments the resulting averages are, unfortunately, not very exact; but the general
character of the results would remain the same even if we
considered the value false within the whole range of the probable error. This character becomes apparent upon comparison
with the values given above (p. 56) for learning by heart six
16-syllable series which had not previously been learned. This
took place in 1,270 seconds. After the original series had been

repeated 16 times, the derived series was learned with a saving of about 100 seconds; after repetition 64 times, with a like saving of 161 seconds. Quadrupling the repetitions resulted in increasing the saving only a little more than half as much again. The increase in strength of the associations reaching over an intermediate member was in nowise proportional to the number of repetitions, for the cases studied, not even within the limits for which this was noticeably the case for associations from one member to its immediate successor. On the contrary the effect of the repetitions in the case of associations of indirect sequence decreased considerably sooner and more quickly than in the case of those of direct sequence.

There is very close agreement between the pair of values just found and the number given above (p. 99, 1)—the procedure being, as here, without the exclusion of knowledge—for the learning of derived series which the day before had been learned in their original form to the point of first possible reproduction. This number, it is true, was obtained under somewhat different conditions. In the first place, not always were the same number of repetitions employed for learning, but each time as many as were required for the first possible reproduction—*i.e.*, not exactly, but on the average, 32. Moreover, the nature of the derivation of the series was somewhat different, as was stated above. But these differences have little weight in the case of numbers which otherwise could have little claim to exactness. I adduce therefore this value for comparison, and in addition the numbers given in Chapter VI for the influence of repetitions on the relearning of the same untransformed series. Here then is the table.

| Number of Repetitions | Time for relearning the untransformed series after 24 hours | Time for relearning after 24 hours series transformed by skipping one syllable | Saving in relearning unchanged series | Saving in learning the changed series | Saving in changed series in % of the saving for the unchanged |
|---|---|---|---|---|---|
| 0 | 1270 | | | | |
| 16 | 1078 | 1170 | 192 | 100 | 52% |
| 32 | 863 | 1121 | 407 | 149 | 37% |
| 64 | 454 | 1109 | 816 | 161 | 20% |

(The numbers of the four intermediate columns mean seconds.)

I call attention again to the fact that the numbers given above are in part rather inexact and that they were gained under very limited conditions. However, it is allowable to sketch summarily and with hypothetical elaboration the view which these results make appear to be the most probable explanation of an important group of inner processes and which fills pleasingly and completely a hitherto empty place in our knowledge.

With the imprinting and internal fixation of an idea-series through its manifold repetition, inner connections, associations, are woven between all the separate members of the series. The nature of these is such that series made out of members thus associated are picked up and reproduced more easily, with less resistance to be overcome, than similar series made up of members not previously associated. Their nature can also be stated in this way, that each member of the series has the definite tendency on its own return to consciousness to bring back others with it. These connections, or tendencies, are of different strength from several different points of view. For the more distant members of the original series they are weaker than for the nearer; for specific distances backwards they are weaker than for the same distances forward. The strength of all the connections increases as the number of repetitions increases. But the originally stronger threads between the nearer members are strengthened considerably more quickly than the weaker ones which connect the more distant terms. The more, therefore, the number of repetitions increases, the stronger, both absolutely and relatively, become the connections between immediately successive terms. To the same degree the more exclusive and dominant becomes the tendency of each term at its own return into consciousness to draw after itself that term which had always immediately followed it during the repetitions.

## Section 42. *Indirect Strengthening of Associations*

I conclude with the mention of a noteworthy fact which appeared incidentally in connection with the investigations mentioned in the preceding paragraphs. On account of the uncertainty of the numerical results which come into consideration, I can call attention to it only with great reserve. I cannot, however, pass it by altogether because it is probable in itself, and because, with further confirmation, it will throw a characteristic light on inner processes which are actually present but which remain unconscious. It will also reveal the relative independence of these processes from conscious accompaniments, as I have shown above (§ 24).

The derivation of the transformed series in the case of the last mentioned investigations was accomplished, as has been stated, in the following way. Out of two 16-syllable series selected by chance, first all the odd-numbered syllables were combined to form a new series and then all the even-numbered to form a second series which followed in immediate succession. In the case of a group consisting of six series of this sort, therefore, the derived series II contained nothing but syllables which in the first process of memorising had followed immediately upon the corresponding members of series I. The derived series IV bore a similar relation to series III, and series VI to series V. The following phenomenon appeared, which is the peculiar relation to which I wish to call attention. Less time was required for learning by heart series II, IV, VI on the average than for series I, III, V, although in all the other groups of series, whether original or derived, the converse was the case.

I adduce some numerical data in evidence of this relation.

From all the experiments with six series of 16 syllables which were learned to the point of the first recital, ten immediately successive experiments are chosen by chance for two different time-periods. The times for committing to memory series I, III, V are combined in calculation, as are also those for series II, IV, VI.

1

| A<br>Sum of series<br>(I, III, V) | B<br>Sum of series<br>(II, IV, VI) | $\Delta$<br>(B–A) |
|---|---|---|
| 467 | 790 | 323 |
| 544 | 666 | 122 |
| 662 | 704 | 42 |
| 548 | 668 | 120 |
| 523 | 539 | 16 |
| 475 | 657 | 182 |
| 612 | 753 | 141 |
| 853 | 548 | —305 |
| 637 | 641 | 4 |
| 499 | 780 | 281 |
| *m* 582 | 675 | 93<br>P.E.$_m$=±37 |

2

| | | |
|---|---|---|
| 488 | 694 | 206 |
| 604 | 704 | 100 |
| 551 | 734 | 183 |
| 596 | 637 | 41 |
| 559 | 686 | 127 |
| 611 | 744 | 133 |
| 653 | 682 | 129 |
| 598 | 700 | 102 |
| 723 | 606 | —117 |
| 643 | 678 | 35 |
| *m* 603 | 687 | 84<br>P.E.$_m$=±20 |

The sum of series II, IV and VI, found by averaging the ten experiments, is here in both cases, as can readily be seen, considerably greater than the sum of series I, III, V. The differences are, to be sure, of very different amounts for the separate experiments, and in one case they have a pronounced negative value; but these fluctuations are represented in the large probable error of the differences of the averages; and, in spite of the size of these errors, the positive character of the differences may be considered as fairly certain.

In all other investigated cases the following result appears: there are large fluctuations of the differences in the individual experiments, but a combination of the several experiments shows a decisive predominance for series II, IV, VI although the surplus is smaller than in the case of the two experiments in question. Thus in the case of 11 earlier tests in which series were learned by heart which had been derived by skipping one intermediate syllable and which had been learned the day before in the original form the results were (p. 99, 1):

Sum of series (II, IV, VI) minus Sum of series (I, III, V) $= 33$ (P.E.$_m = 23$).

With six later tests of the same sort (p. 103, 1):

Sum of (II, IV, VI) minus Sum of (I, III, V) $= 42$ (P.E.$_m = 29$).

With ten experiments with series which had been repeated the day before 16 times each (p. 55):

Sum of (II, IV, VI) minus Sum of (I, III, V) $= 17$ (P.E.$_m = 21$), etc.

On account of the largeness of the probable error a single one of the last given figures would have little significance. By means of their correspondence as to the nature of the difference they gain in probability, and the phenomenon becomes quite intelligible in light of the results of Section 18. There, and with especial clearness in the case of 16-syllable series, it was shown that the learning of the individual series occurred in the form of fairly regular oscillations. These were of such a sort that a relatively slowly learned series followed one learned relatively more quickly and vice versa (p. 43, Fig. 3). Since in the case of each experiment the first series was learned on the average the most quickly and the second the most slowly, by the combination of series I, III, V the average minima are united and of series II, IV, VI the average maxima. The difference, $S$ (II, IV, VI) minus (I, III, V) is, therefore, in general positive.

Accordingly it must be surprising that in the case of both the groups of tests mentioned in the preceding paragraphs, this difference is on the contrary of a negative sign.

(1) The results in the case of learning derived series which had been repeated 16 times on the day previous in their original form were as follows:

| A<br>Sum of<br>(I, III, V) | B<br>Sum of<br>(II, IV, VI) | *Δ*<br>(B–A) |
|---|---|---|
| 656 | 522 | —134 |
| 702 | 514 | —188 |
| 603 | 613 | 10 |
| 450 | 500 | 50 |
| 662 | 696 | 34 |
| 560 | 459 | —101 |
| 588 | 603 | 15 |
| 637 | 593 | —44 |
| Av. 607 | 562 | —45 P.E.m ±21 |

(2) The results of learning derived series which had been repeated 64 times on the day previous in their original form were as follows:

| A<br>Sum of<br>(I, III, V) | B<br>Sum of<br>(II, IV, VI) | *Δ*<br>(B–A) |
|---|---|---|
| 515 | 642 | 127 |
| 567 | 415 | —152 |
| 626 | 572 | —54 |
| 588 | 560 | —28 |
| 543 | 452 | —91 |
| 539 | 478 | —61 |
| 584 | 599 | 15 |
| 592 | 604 | 12 |
| Av. 569 | 540 | —29 P.E.m ±20 |

The fluctuations of the numbers for the separate experiments are also in this case very great. However, it is evident on the first glance and without further comparison that a strong displacement of the differences to the negative side has taken place. This fact is also expressed by the averages. In contrast with previous results, the series II, IV, VI were learned in somewhat shorter time than series I, III, V.

That this exception rests on mere chance is possible but not very probable. The probable errors, although large, are not large enough to indicate this.

I would sooner fear that it was a case of disturbance of the results through the oft-mentioned source of error, anticipation of the outcome (p. 27 ff. and p. 101). During the progress of the experiment I believed with increasing certainty that I could fore-

see the smaller expenditure of time for the learning of series II,
IV, VI, and it was only because I thought something of this
sort that I changed the method of derivation of the transformed
series.   I cannot, therefore, exclude the possibility that, merely
on the basis of this hidden presupposition and in a manner
altogether unrevealed to consciousness, a greater concentration
of attention was present in learning series II, IV, VI than in
learning series I, III, V.   However, this assumption is not to
be taken positively as the correct one.   The assumption that the
whole of the difference found is to be traced back to the influence of this source of error would involve the ascription of a
pretty large function to an involuntary and completely unconscious accommodation of attention due to a secret expectation.

There remains, accordingly, a certain probability for the third
possibility, namely, that the contrasting character of the average
differences has in part at least an objective basis, that the more
rapid learning of the derived series, II, IV, VI, was in part
due to their manner of derivation.

The proper way in which to think of this causation would
become clear only by the introduction of physiological conceptions which must first be constructed or at least remodelled.
If use is made of the language of psychology, then, as in the
case of all unconscious processes, expression can be only figurative and inexact.

As a result of the learning by heart of a series in the original
form the separate syllables, we must say, retain fairly strong
tendencies upon their own return to consciousness to bring after
them the syllables which immediately succeeded them.   If, therefore, the syllables 1, 3, 5, etc., return to consciousness, the
syllables 2, 4, 6, etc., have a tendency also to appear.   This
tendency is not strong enough to bring about as a consciously
perceivable event the actual appearance of 2, 4, 6.   The latter
are in evidence only in a certain inner condition of excitability;
something takes place in them which would not have occurred
if 1, 3, 5 had not been repeated.   They behave like a forgotten
name which one attempts to recollect.   This is not consciously
present; on the contrary, it is being sought.   In a certain way,
however, it is undeniably present.   It is on the way to consciousness, as one might say.   For if ideas of all sorts were
called up which stood in connection with the earlier experienced

name, a person could usually tell whether they agreed with the one now sought for but not yet found, or not. As a result of the frequent repetition of the syllables 1, 3, 5 previously connected with the syllables 2, 4, 6, the latter were placed in a similar slightly pronounced condition of excitation, lying between conscious appearance on the one side and simple non-appearance on the other. And this excitation has, as it now appears from our tests, a result altogether similar to that of actual return to consciousness. Inner connections are established between successively and internally aroused syllables just as between syllables successively raised to consciousness, except that the former are naturally of less strength. Secret threads are spun which bind together the series 2, 4, 6, not yet aroused to consciousness, and prepare the way for its conscious appearance. Such threads existed already in greater strength as a result of the learning of the original series; the present effect is that of strengthening somewhat connections already made. And that is nothing else than what was found above: if two syllable-combinations—1, 3, 5 . . . and 2, 4, 6 . . . —are frequently associated in consciousness (the learning of the original series) then the subsequent learning of the second combination (derived series II, IV, VI) soon after the learning of the first (derived series I, III, V) has considerably less resistance to overcome than the latter. A certain strengthening of associations takes place, not only directly, through conscious repetition of the associated members, but also indirectly through the conscious repetition of other members with which the first had been frequently connected.

This way of viewing the matter is a consequence of the assumption (which became necessary above, p. 109) of the formation of associative connections over more intervening members than could be comprehended in one clearly conscious act. These connections would be very fruitful in the explanation of many surprising phenomena of memory and recollection, but on account of the uncertainty of their experiential basis I refrain for the present from pursuing them further.

12653175R00074

Printed in Great Britain
by Amazon.co.uk, Ltd.,
Marston Gate.